The Children's Book of ANIMALS AROUND US

Written by
Bridget Gibbs, Su Swallow and
Ruth Thomson

Consultant Editors
Angela Bell, Public Relations Officer of the
British Goat Society; George Fleetwood of the
Rural Studies Department, Burford School;
Keith Fowler, Farm Manager of Cobbs Wood
Farm; L.B. Halstead, Ph.D., D.Sc., of the
University of Reading; Peter Messent, M.A.,
D.Phil., of Pedigree Petfoods; Patricia Scott,
M.B.E. Ph.D., F.I. Biol., of the University of
London; Joanna Spector; Hilary Tinley of
The Association of Agriculture

Designed by
Sally Burrough

Edited by
Bridget Gibbs and Roz Kidman-Cox

Illustrated by
John Barber, Joyce Bee, John Francis,
Colin King, Malcolm McGregor,
Andy Martin, Robert Morton, Sam Peffer

Printed in Belgium by Henri Proost, Turnhout, Belgium.

Acknowledgements
We wish to thank the
following organizations for
their assistance and for
making available material in
their collections:

Arbour Acres (UK) Ltd.
The Association of Agriculture
The Australian High
  Commission (Canberra
  House)
The Australian Meat and
  Live-Stock Corporation
The Belgian Embassy
The British Briard Club
The British Goat Society
The British Museum
The British Poultry Meat
  Association
The British Turkey Federation
Cherry Valley Farms
The Cheviot Sheep Society

Chorley Chicks Ltd.
Cobb Breeding Company
Dairy Farmer
The Dorset Down
  Sheepbreeders' Association
The Dorset Horn
  Sheepbreeders' Association
Farmers' Weekly
Greyhound Magazine
The Guide Dogs for the Blind
  Association
The Hampshire Down
  Sheepbreeders' Association
Hubbard Poultry (UK) Ltd.
The Meat and Livestock
  Commission
The Milk Marketing Board
The National Farmers' Union
The National Pig Breeders'
  Association
Pedigree Petfoods Education
  Centre

The Poultry Research Centre
Poultry World
The Royal Society for the
  Prevention of Cruelty to
  Animals
The Shire Horse Society
Southdown Hatcheries Ltd.
The Southdown Sheep
  Society
Swift Poultry Company

The Children's Book of ANIMALS AROUND US

Contents

Silver Tabby

Seal-pointed Siamese

Part 1 written by
Bridget Gibbs

2

Part 1 CATS

This section will help you to understand how cats behave and how to look after a cat of your own. It explains why cats do curious things like eating wool and what it means when a cat swishes its tail or flattens its ears. It also looks at the parts of a cat's body and shows how they work and what happens as a cat gets older.

If you do not have a cat of your own but would like to get one, the information on pages 24-27 will help you to choose a healthy kitten and learn how to look after and train it.

The chart on pages 30-31 shows many of the different kinds of pedigree cats. You can use it to help you make a survey of the cats in your area, as described on page 29.

If you are interested in finding out more about pedigree cats or in joining a cat club, it is best to go to a few cat shows.

At a show you will be able to ask about cat clubs. You can join a club even if you have a mongrel cat, and some people join a club without even having a cat. All clubs have regular meetings with guest speakers. By going to these meetings you will learn much more about how to look after your cat properly.

Red Self

The world of cats

The domestic cat belongs to the animal family called Felidae, which includes all cats from large ones such as lions to smaller ones such as lynxes. Cats are carnivores, or meat-eaters. All carnivores developed from a weasel-like ancestor called Miacis.

The cat-like animals that descended from Miacis, which lived on earth millions of years before man, were the ancestors of all the cats we know today. No-one is quite sure how cats eventually came to be tamed, or domesticated, but it is likely that they have been associated with man from about the time he started farming. The ancient Egyptians, who lived about 4,000 years ago, may have been the first people to be aware of the cat's usefulness. They probably started to feed cats as a reward for ridding their homes of mice, which were eating their grain.

The cat family are hunters, relying on stealth and speed to catch and kill their prey. Several features enable them to be excellent hunters: they have supple joints, powerful muscles, special teeth and sharp, retractable claws (see page 7).

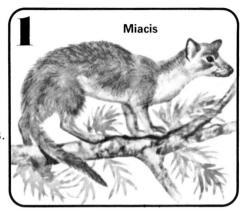

About 50 million years ago, a small weasel-like creature called Miacis lived by hunting prey in the forests. It was the ancestor of all living carnivores.

An animal called Dinictis developed, or evolved, from Miacis about 36 million years ago. It looked a bit like a lynx, and had cat-like teeth and claws.

All present-day cats belong to the cat family (Felidae), which evolved from Dinictis. The wild cat shown here lives in European forests.

The domestic cat is probably descended from the desert cats of Egypt and Arabia. These cats tame easily and would accept domestic life more readily than any others.

Big cats

The cheetah is the only cat which has claws that cannot be retracted (sheathed) when they are not in use.

Most cats except lions prefer to live and hunt on their own. Lions live in family groups called prides.

Skulls and teeth

The sabre-toothed tiger, called Smilodon, was a descendant of Miacis and lived about the same time as Dinictis. It, too, was a carnivore and it had enormous canine teeth for catching and killing prey. Like Dinictis it had eyes and ears well placed at the front of its head for detecting prey.

Modern cats, including the domestic cat, have essentially the same features as their ancestors for catching, killing and eating prey. They have forward facing eyes, a strong hinged lower jaw, large, sharp canine teeth and tearing carnassial teeth.

The cat's skeleton

A cat's skeleton is made up of about 230 bones which are worked by about 500 muscles. Unlike dogs, whose skeletons vary considerably in shape and size, all domestic cat skeletons are very similar. They are lightly built and so flexible that, unlike humans' limbs, the cat's limbs do not get put out of joint.

Cats walk differently from other animals. Their front legs swing inwards so that the feet land in a line, one in front of the other, directly under the cat's body. The hind legs do not swing in quite so much, but the footprints still nearly overlap. This is why cats can walk along fences and narrow ledges.

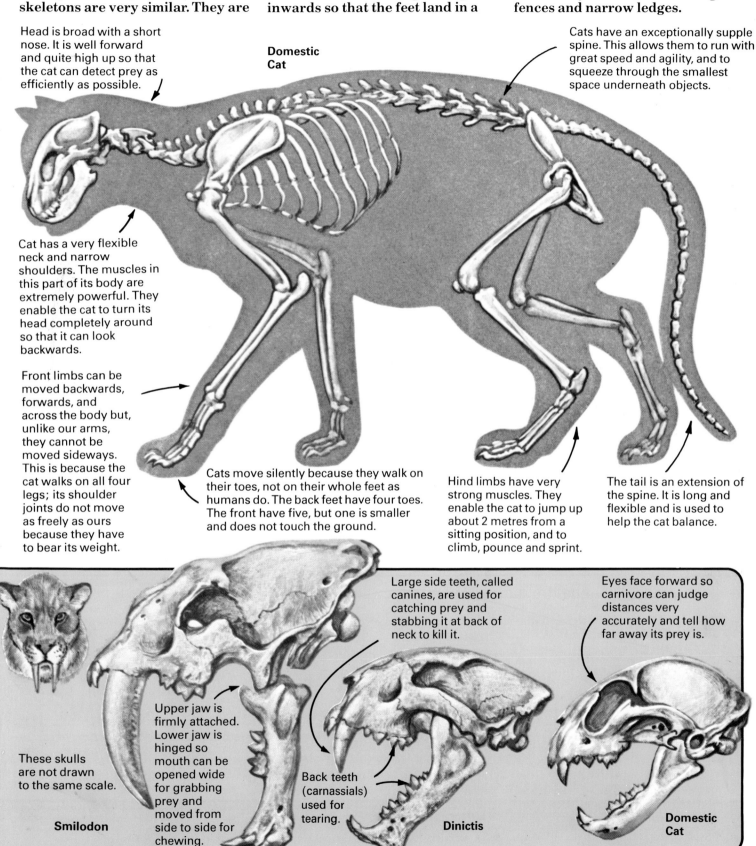

Head is broad with a short nose. It is well forward and quite high up so that the cat can detect prey as efficiently as possible.

Domestic Cat

Cats have an exceptionally supple spine. This allows them to run with great speed and agility, and to squeeze through the smallest space underneath objects.

Cat has a very flexible neck and narrow shoulders. The muscles in this part of its body are extremely powerful. They enable the cat to turn its head completely around so that it can look backwards.

Front limbs can be moved backwards, forwards, and across the body but, unlike our arms, they cannot be moved sideways. This is because the cat walks on all four legs; its shoulder joints do not move as freely as ours because they have to bear its weight.

Cats move silently because they walk on their toes, not on their whole feet as humans do. The back feet have four toes. The front have five, but one is smaller and does not touch the ground.

Hind limbs have very strong muscles. They enable the cat to jump up about 2 metres from a sitting position, and to climb, pounce and sprint.

The tail is an extension of the spine. It is long and flexible and is used to help the cat balance.

Large side teeth, called canines, are used for catching prey and stabbing it at back of neck to kill it.

Eyes face forward so carnivore can judge distances very accurately and tell how far away its prey is.

These skulls are not drawn to the same scale.

Upper jaw is firmly attached. Lower jaw is hinged so mouth can be opened wide for grabbing prey and moved from side to side for chewing.

Back teeth (carnassials) used for tearing.

Smilodon

Dinictis

Domestic Cat

A cat's body

Cats spend much of their time asleep, but when they feel like it, they can move with lightning speed. They are among the top ten all-round athletes of the animal world. Cats have amazingly flexible bodies, but you may wonder how they manage to keep so fit when they take so little exercise. The answer lies largely in the lengthy stretching routine they go through on waking. This involves a whole series of leg, paw and back stretching movements, beginning with an upright thrust, that arches the cat's back.

The cat's body shape has developed for pouncing, springing, jumping, climbing and sprinting. Cats are perfectly equipped for fast, short runs but their heart and lungs are not built to cope with the "staying power" needed for longer runs.

Fur is the main feature that distinguishes one cat from another. All kittens have soft downy fur, but between four and six months old, the adult coat grows and noticeably changes their appearance. A cat's fur may be long or short, all one colour or a mixture of several.

Cats are very good at balancing on narrow ledges such as garden fences. Their powerful muscles, light bones and flexible joints make them very agile and their sharp claws help them to grip well.

The muscles of a cat's body must co-ordinate (work together), when it jumps from any height down to the ground. The positioning of the tail, head and limbs is specially important.

A cat can bend its spine almost double, enabling it to wash around the base of its tail. Notice how it twists its body to balance in this position with one leg in the air.

Making paw prints

TUBE OF LINO-PRINTING INK (DARK COLOUR)

SHEET OF GLASS

ROLL INK ONTO GLASS

WHITE PAPER

INKED GLASS

FINISHED PRINT

You can make prints of cats' paws in the following way:

Spread a thin line of non-toxic printing ink on a sheet of glass, or other smooth surface. Roll out the ink on the glass with a printing roller, or spread it evenly with a brush. Put the glass on the floor surrounded by sheets of white paper. Place the cat gently on the inked surface. The cat will walk off the glass onto the paper (try bribing it with a bowl of food), leaving sets of paw prints.

Notice the difference between the back and front paws, and compare your cat's prints with those of other cats.

Tongue, teeth, whiskers

A cat's tongue is long and thin, and extremely versatile. One moment it may be used for lapping milk, its edges curled up like a spoon, and the next it is being used for grooming the cat's fur.

If a cat licks your hand, you will notice how rough its tongue feels. The tongue's surface is covered with small, backward-pointing projections, called papillae, and these act like a comb when the cat licks its fur. Cats also use their tongues for tasting; they are sensitive to salt, sour and bitter tastes, and possibly to water.

Cats have long, sharp canine teeth, which are used for catching and killing prey. They are also used in grooming, to tease out

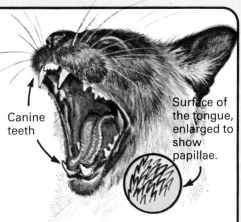

Canine teeth

Surface of the tongue, enlarged to show papillae.

knotted hair or dirt. Their back teeth are used for chewing. The front teeth, or incisors, are very small and are not used much. Old cats' incisors may drop out.

Cats' whiskers are very sensitive. They act as feelers and help the cat avoid obstacles.

Fur

Base of a single hair, enlarged.

Skin

Hair

Hair muscle

Fur is a waterproof covering which protects the cat's body from bites and scratches, and from getting too hot or cold. Most cats have two kinds of hair, downy underhairs and coarse overhairs or guard hairs. The guard hairs are sensitive, like whiskers, and enable the cat to feel pain and pleasure.

Cats can use their fur to make themselves look larger and more threatening. Each guard hair has a muscle attached to it and when this tightens, the hair stands on end.

Eyes

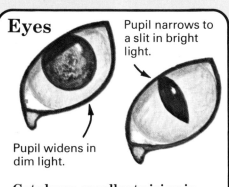

Pupil narrows to a slit in bright light.

Pupil widens in dim light.

Cats have excellent vision in daylight, but really unique vision at night when most of their hunting is done. Special tissue at the back of the eye enables them to use very dim light that is useless to humans.

Ears

Ears turn to face direction of sound, and can move separately.

Cats can hear sounds that are higher-pitched and softer than the ones we can hear. Their ears can move faster than dogs' ears, and they can quickly pick up sounds from a particular direction. The ears also express feelings, such as aggression (see page 9).

Tail

The long, flexible tail is an extension of the cat's spine. It is an important balancing aid and is held out behind when the cat jumps or springs. It can tell you a lot about a cat's mood (see page 9).

Claws and paws

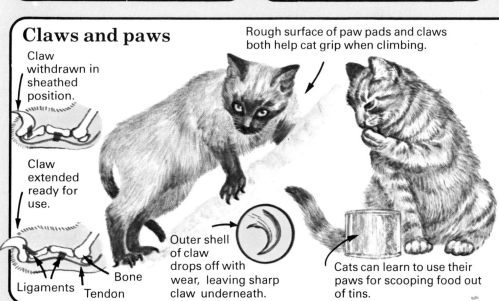

Claw withdrawn in sheathed position.

Claw extended ready for use.

Ligaments   Bone   Tendon

Rough surface of paw pads and claws both help cat grip when climbing.

Outer shell of claw drops off with wear, leaving sharp claw underneath.

Cats can learn to use their paws for scooping food out of tins.

Cats' paws are used for climbing, feeding, washing, digging, hunting and playing. The cushioned paw pads enable a cat to walk silently, land safely when jumping, and also to feel, as they are very sensitive.

Cats' sharp, curved claws do not get blunt because, unlike dogs' claws (which are always visible), they are kept sheathed when not in use. To extend the claws, muscles in the cat's leg contract. This tightens the tendons (cord-like bands of tissue) attached to these muscles. The tendons pull down the bones that bear the claws, exposing them.

Cat language

Cats communicate with other cats, other animals and people by means of their own special language. This is made up of a range of sounds, facial expressions and movements, each of which has a precise meaning.

Some cats "talk" more than others, but most can make about 16 different sounds. The most important sounds are miaow, purr, hiss, mutter, growl and yowl. By watching carefully, you can quickly learn to understand what a cat is "saying" when it twitches its tail and mews, or flattens its ears and growls.

The language of smell

Cats also mark out their territory by scratching trees with their front claws, and by rubbing against objects to leave scent from glands on their head.

Cats are very possessive about their home area, or territory. Toms (male cats) and some females mark out their territory regularly by spraying their urine against objects such as trees and shrubs. The urine contains a strong odour which indicates ownership of the area to other cats and warns them against intruding. The dots in the picture show the places which a tom might mark.

Cats have glands, which produce scent, on each side of their forehead, and on their lips, chin and tail. They use scent to show friendship and "ownership." When a friendly cat rubs its head against your legs, it is marking you with scent from the glands on its head. Cats that are friendly will mark one another in the same way. Unlike the scent used to mark territory, we can't smell this.

Cat talk

Growling and hissing are used as threats, to warn other animals, and often other cats, to keep away. A cat may growl and hiss at a strange dog, even if the dog is friendly.

The familiar low, rumbling sound of a cat purring is a sign of contentment or pleasure. No-one is quite sure how this sound is made, but you can feel the vibrations if you touch a cat's throat on its voice-box, or put your hand on its chest.

A cat will miaow loudly when it wants something, such as food or to be let outside. This is an unmistakably demanding sound. Cats can express many different needs by varying the tone of their miaows.

A lazily contented cat will roll over onto its back and lie with its front limbs bent and its eyes half-closed. Exposing its belly is a sign of trust and security.

A cat will run to greet its owner with its tail held up like this.

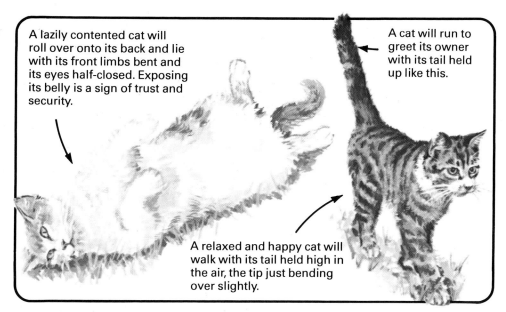

A relaxed and happy cat will walk with its tail held high in the air, the tip just bending over slightly.

An inquisitive cat pricks its ears, listening for sounds. As it concentrates on the object of interest, its pupils widen and its whiskers lift and twitch.

Body language

Cats express their feelings with their whole bodies, especially with their face and tail. They normally use body language more than sound when they are "talking" to one another. Sounds are used mainly when they are with people.

Watch a cat's face and see how its eyes vary from being half-closed with contentment to wide open with fear or surprise. Its ears may be laid back flat in anger or fear, or pricked in curiosity. Its tail may be held erect in friendship or lashing from side to side in anger. Notice that it is the precise combination of ear, eye, mouth and whisker movements used together with the body and tail movements that express the cat's feelings.

When annoyed or irritated, a cat stands stiff-legged, swishing its tail from side to side. The pupils of its eyes widen slightly.

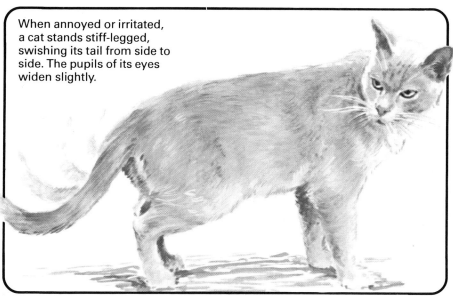

If a cat is threatened by another cat it tries to make itself look as frightening as possible. It raises its fur and bushes out its tail to make itself look larger. It also flattens its ears, widens its pupils, extends its claws and draws back its lips, revealing its teeth.

A frightened cat, cornered by a dog, will crouch with its back arched. Its whiskers and ears will be held back and it may raise a paw, ready to defend itself.

When two friendly cats meet, they greet each other by touching whiskers and noses, sniffing the areas where there are scent glands.

Hunting

All members of the cat family are carnivores (meat-eating animals). Their structure and behaviour have developed over thousands of years to make them almost perfect hunters. They are able to stalk their prey silently, creeping forward on their padded feet, and then pounce on the unsuspecting victim using their sharp claws and teeth for seizing and killing it.

The ability to hunt is instinctive or natural to all cats. Even domestic cats, which do not need to live by hunting prey, have the same instincts. Cats' skill at hunting is made possible by their well-developed sight and hearing. (Dogs, on the other hand, rely more on the sense of smell).

The simple tests on this page show that if you imitate the sound and movement of a cat's prey, the cat will begin stalking the "prey," even though it is only make-believe.

Kittens start play-hunting when they are about six weeks old, stalking and pouncing on one another. But they learn to kill and eat prey by experience, usually by watching their mother.

Stalking and killing

1 When a cat spots a small animal, such as a mouse, it will freeze in a crouched position close to the ground, with its tail tip twitching in excitement. It watches the prey carefully to get an idea of its speed and to see in which direction it is moving.

Learning to hunt

Kittens love to stalk and ambush one another. They will chase and pounce on anything that moves, even dead leaves blown by the wind. It is through these games that kittens develop hunting skills.

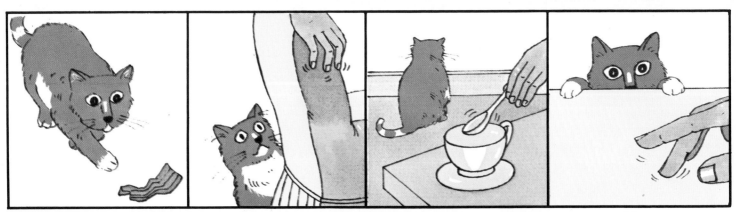

Cats are attracted to rustling and scratching noises which sound like small animals scurrying about in dead leaves or long grass. Swift movement also attracts a cat's attention.

Try to find out which noises and movements attract your cat, and watch it stalking the "prey." Crinkle up a small piece of paper or silver foil and toss it on the floor. Scratch your finger nails on carpet or chair covers. Tap a spoon on a cup. Tip-toe your fingers across the top of a table. Notice that the cat may look up when you tap the cup but it will not start to stalk.

10

2

Having studied its prey, the cat then begins its attack. It moves forward quickly in a low stalking run, with its tail swishing gently.

3

As the cat nears the prey, it prepares to pounce. Its hind legs push back and its bottom is raised up and begins to sway from side to side, while its tail twitches more wildly.

4

The cat springs forward, reaching out with its front paws to pin down the prey. As it seizes the prey, the cat spreads its hind legs further apart to act as a brake.

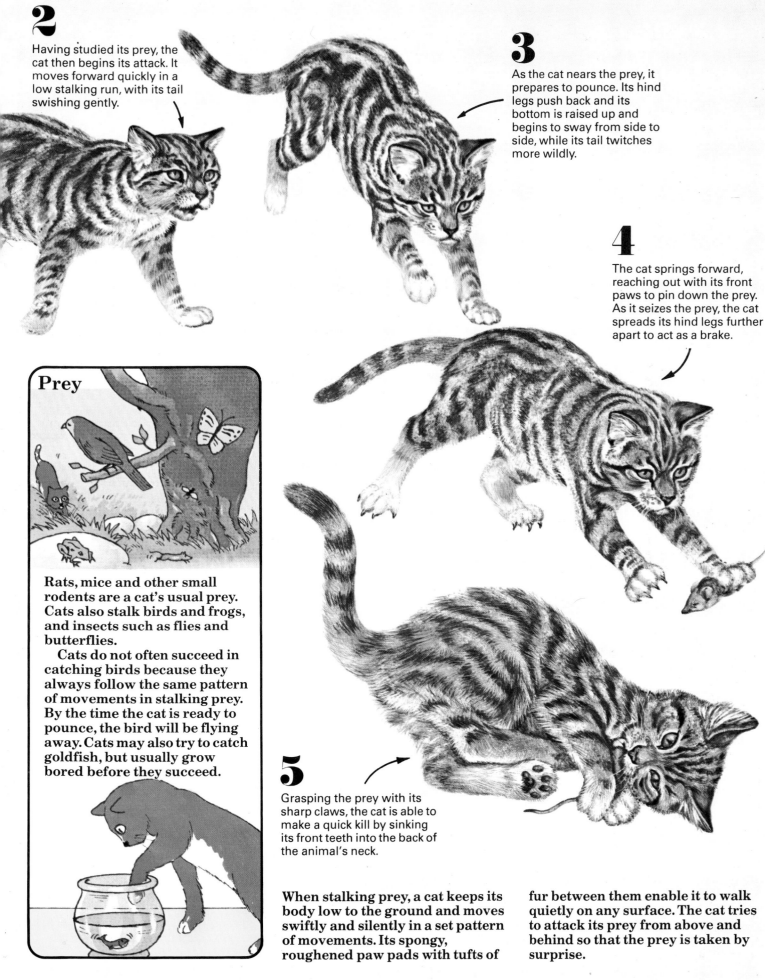

Prey

Rats, mice and other small rodents are a cat's usual prey. Cats also stalk birds and frogs, and insects such as flies and butterflies.

Cats do not often succeed in catching birds because they always follow the same pattern of movements in stalking prey. By the time the cat is ready to pounce, the bird will be flying away. Cats may also try to catch goldfish, but usually grow bored before they succeed.

5

Grasping the prey with its sharp claws, the cat is able to make a quick kill by sinking its front teeth into the back of the animal's neck.

When stalking prey, a cat keeps its body low to the ground and moves swiftly and silently in a set pattern of movements. Its spongy, roughened paw pads with tufts of fur between them enable it to walk quietly on any surface. The cat tries to attack its prey from above and behind so that the prey is taken by surprise.

How cats behave

Cats spend most of their time grooming and washing, or sleeping. They are extremely particular about keeping clean and always wash after a meal and when they wake up. In grooming, they use their tongues to "comb" their fur, and their teeth to tease out any knotted hair or dirt. Grooming also often expresses a cat's feelings. It may be a sign of friendship, embarrassment or aloofness.

Cats show a natural curiosity and will investigate any object they find lying around. Often such objects make good play-things, especially if the cat can dive inside or if the object is small enough to be moved around.

Play is particularly important in the first few weeks of a cat's life. It is largely through playing that kittens learn how to hunt for food, and how to escape from enemies and defend themselves.

Cats are friendly, peace-loving animals and will usually run away from an enemy rather than become involved in a fight. But cats, especially tomcats, are possessive about their own territory. They will become very aggressive towards intruders.

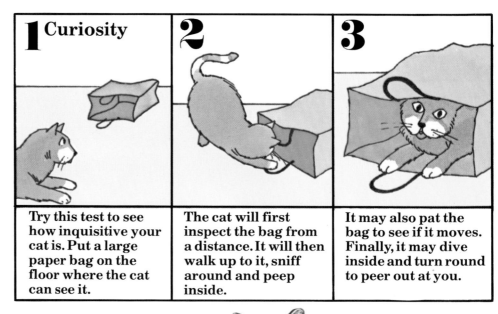

1 Curiosity

Try this test to see how inquisitive your cat is. Put a large paper bag on the floor where the cat can see it.

2

The cat will first inspect the bag from a distance. It will then walk up to it, sniff around and peep inside.

3

It may also pat the bag to see if it moves. Finally, it may dive inside and turn round to peer out at you.

Sleeping

Much of a cat's sleep is a very light sleep, called a cat nap, from which the cat can wake instantly. Cats will nap in odd places, often perched on ledges.

Cats sleep soundly only when they feel secure, in their own box or on a favourite chair. During this deep sleep, cats may dream. Their limbs and faces twitch and they may make little muttering noises.

1 Grooming and washing

A cat can twist its head right round over its shoulder to wash and groom the side of its body.

2

Cats use their forepaws to wash their faces and ears. First, they lick the paw well to moisten it.

The damp paw is then wiped across the cat's face in a sweeping movement from the ear down to the chin.

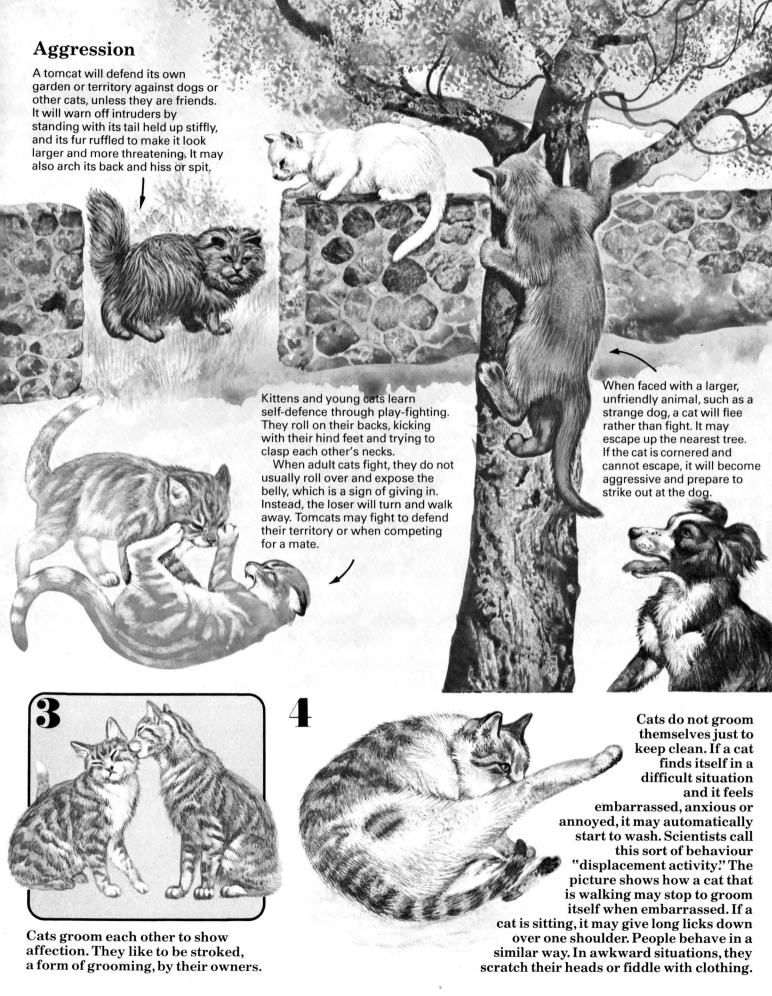

Aggression

A tomcat will defend its own garden or territory against dogs or other cats, unless they are friends. It will warn off intruders by standing with its tail held up stiffly, and its fur ruffled to make it look larger and more threatening. It may also arch its back and hiss or spit.

Kittens and young cats learn self-defence through play-fighting. They roll on their backs, kicking with their hind feet and trying to clasp each other's necks.

When adult cats fight, they do not usually roll over and expose the belly, which is a sign of giving in. Instead, the loser will turn and walk away. Tomcats may fight to defend their territory or when competing for a mate.

When faced with a larger, unfriendly animal, such as a strange dog, a cat will flee rather than fight. It may escape up the nearest tree. If the cat is cornered and cannot escape, it will become aggressive and prepare to strike out at the dog.

3

Cats groom each other to show affection. They like to be stroked, a form of grooming, by their owners.

4

Cats do not groom themselves just to keep clean. If a cat finds itself in a difficult situation and it feels embarrassed, anxious or annoyed, it may automatically start to wash. Scientists call this sort of behaviour "displacement activity." The picture shows how a cat that is walking may stop to groom itself when embarrassed. If a cat is sitting, it may give long licks down over one shoulder. People behave in a similar way. In awkward situations, they scratch their heads or fiddle with clothing.

Intelligence and learning

Cats have exceptional abilities and highly developed senses which, in the past, led people to believe that they had magical powers. Even now, many people still believe that cats have a "sixth sense." However, research by scientists shows that it is the exceptionally acute senses and high level of intelligence that enables cats to perform apparently amazing feats.

Three kinds of behaviour

Cats show three different kinds of behaviour. The simplest of these is involuntary or reflex behaviour, such as flicking an ear when the hairs around it are touched. People show these reflex actions too. If you touch something very hot, for example, you automatically let it go before you feel pain.

Instincts

The second kind of behaviour is instinctive. Most of a kitten's early activities are instinctive responses to its environment. For example, newborn kittens instinctively react to the smell of milk and suckle from their mother, and a litter of kittens instinctively huddles together for warmth when their mother leaves the nest.

Learning and memory

The third kind of behaviour is the result of experience. A cat learns by imitating its mother, other cats or even humans, and also by trial and error. As kittens grow up, more of their behaviour is guided by learning and memory, but basic instincts are still important.

Opening windows

Cats are lovers of freedom and dislike being shut up in enclosed spaces. Many learn to open windows and doors so that they can come and go as they please.

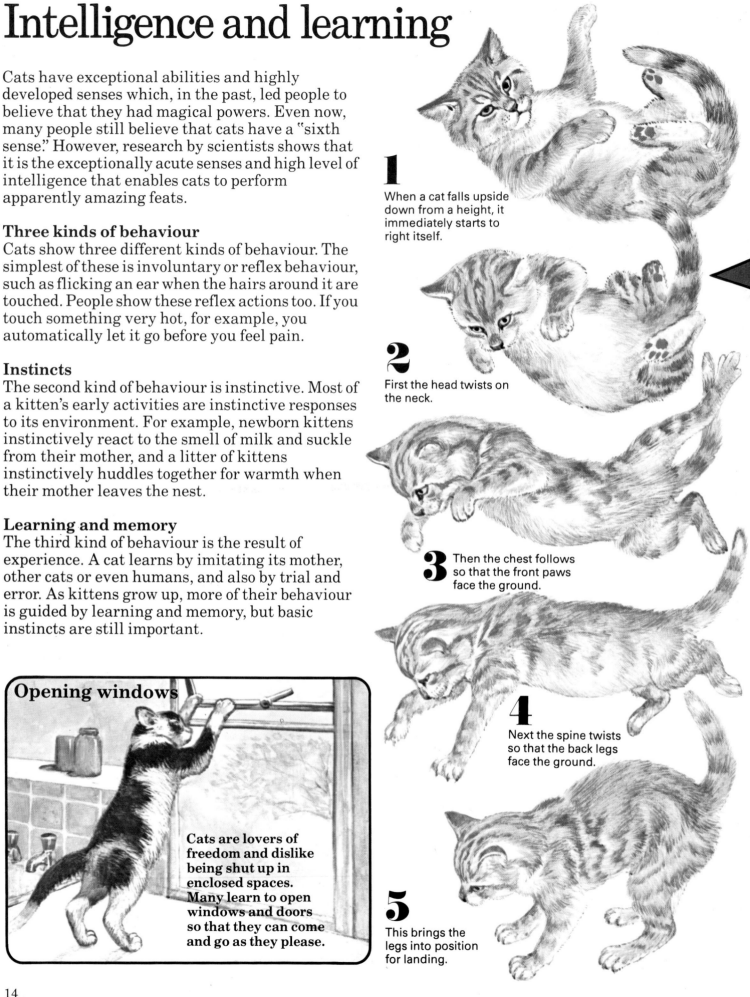

1 When a cat falls upside down from a height, it immediately starts to right itself.

2 First the head twists on the neck.

3 Then the chest follows so that the front paws face the ground.

4 Next the spine twists so that the back legs face the ground.

5 This brings the legs into position for landing.

Falling

Cats have a remarkable sense of balance and more flexible bodies than dogs. If a cat falls upside down from a height, it will twist its head and body in an orderly series of movements so that it lands safely on its feet. This is a reflex action, called the righting reflex.

REMEMBER!
CATS ARE VERY INDEPENDENT AND DO NOT LIKE BEING HANDLED ROUGHLY OR BEING DROPPED. THEY HAVE GOOD MEMORIES AND BECOME WARY OF ANYONE WHO MISTREATS THEM.

Homing ability

Cats are able to find their way back to their own home territory even when they are some distance away from home, as when their owners move house and take them to live in a new area. Some cats have been known to travel hundreds of kilometres to return home. They may be able to tell which direction to travel from the position of the sun in the sky.

Usually, cats can only find their way home over much shorter distances. The actual distance is thought to depend on the cat's ability to recognize its surroundings. City cats have small territories and are not used to wandering far. They can only

find their way home from about one to two kilometres away. Country cats nearly always have larger territories and can get home from distances of up to 16 kilometres.

Time sense

Cats have a very strong sense of time. Wild members of the cat family learn the movements of animals around them and the best time of day to go hunting. Similarly, domestic cats learn to fit their daily habits into their owner's routine and know when to expect food. Some cats learn their owner's routine so well that they will wake them a few minutes before the alarm clock rings in the morning.

Recognizing familiar sounds

Many cats are able to detect their owner's arrival long before anyone else is aware that the person is near. This is because they have excellent hearing and can learn to distinguish their owner's footsteps from all others. Some cats also learn to recognize the sound of their owner's car engine.

Because they are intelligent, cats quickly learn how to get the things they want. A cat that accidentally knocks over a milk jug will drink the milk that spills out. When the cat next sees a jug it may deliberately knock it over. The cat has learned that the jug is a likely source of food. This is one reason why cats should never be allowed onto tables.

Watching cats

Cats eat some kinds of grass, perhaps as a kind of medicine. When they wash, cats swallow some of their fur and this can collect in balls in their stomach. To get rid of these fur balls they eat grass, which makes them sick.

Some cats will eat wool if they are very bored. They start to behave like kittens, kneading with their front paws and sucking at something woollen, such as their own blanket or a pullover. They do this because they want attention and company.

Cats can be jealous of other cats in their own home. If a cat thinks it is getting less than its fair share of attention, it may push in when another is being stroked. It may also try to get attention by rubbing against its owner's legs.

Some cats appear to enjoy watching television with their owners. It is probably the flickering movement of the screen which fascinates them.

Cats sometimes seem to admire themselves in mirrors. They are attracted by the movement they can see. Some cats may even try to look behind a mirror to find the "other cat" they think they have seen.

Cats are amazingly patient. They will spend their time crouching by a mousehole if they can smell mice. This is because cats hunt prey by ambushing it, and learn to wait for the right time to pounce.

Cats that go hunting at night often bring home prey and present it to their owner. This is not done just to "show off." It is based on the natural instinct of a mother cat bringing home prey to her kittens for food.

Most cats do not like getting wet. They seem to have a natural fear of water although they can swim well. But some cats are fascinated by the movement of water and will sit watching a tap drip. Some may even paw at a trickle of water.

Cats can be very aloof. By nature, they are independent animals and please only themselves. Sometimes, a cat may not want to play when you do. It will ignore you and may start washing.

Keeping a record

It is fun to keep a scrap book if you have your own cat. You can make drawings of your cat as it grows up, and take photographs if you have a camera. You may find bits of fur and claws and discarded whiskers you can stick in your book. Make notes about your cat's behaviour, using this book to help you.

Kipper at 8 weeks

Kipper at 6 months old

Kipper at 10 weeks

fur

claws

The ageing cat

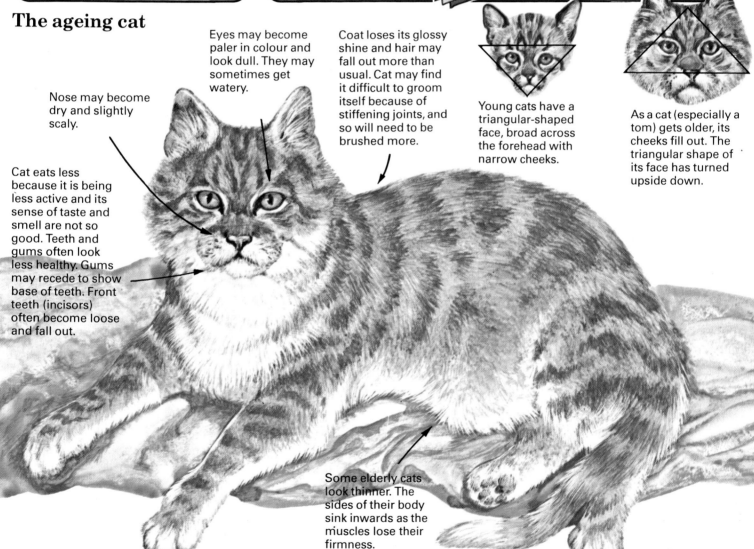

Eyes may become paler in colour and look dull. They may sometimes get watery.

Coat loses its glossy shine and hair may fall out more than usual. Cat may find it difficult to groom itself because of stiffening joints, and so will need to be brushed more.

Nose may become dry and slightly scaly.

Cat eats less because it is being less active and its sense of taste and smell are not so good. Teeth and gums often look less healthy. Gums may recede to show base of teeth. Front teeth (incisors) often become loose and fall out.

Some elderly cats look thinner. The sides of their body sink inwards as the muscles lose their firmness.

Young cats have a triangular-shaped face, broad across the forehead with narrow cheeks.

As a cat (especially a tom) gets older, its cheeks fill out. The triangular shape of its face has turned upside down.

Cats live longer than most other pets, and usually slightly longer than dogs. A cat's average lifespan is about 12 to 15 years, but some cats have lived 30 years. Cats are normally active until they are about 10 or 12 years old. After this, they become less alert. Their sense of balance may not be so good and they move about more slowly. Older cats need to be kept warm. They should be given several small meals a day rather than one or two larger ones and should not be allowed to get too fat. They may want to go outside more often to urinate. These changes are all due to their bodies working less efficiently as they get older.

Courtship and mating

Healthy female kittens can mate and produce kittens of their own when they are only six to eight months old and not yet fully grown. Males take slightly longer to develop. They are usually between nine and fifteen months old when they are first able to mate.

Cats do not usually mate during the shortest days of the year. When the days are longer, in the period from spring to autumn, females have a two to three week pattern or cycle of activity which is repeated continuously. For the first week or so of the cycle, the female is able to mate and is said to be "on heat" or "in season." If she is not mated during this time, a resting phase follows, until the next period of heat about two weeks later.

Females on heat are often courted by several toms if they are allowed to roam freely. A female will mate several times in one heat period, so she may mate with more than one of the toms that court her. She rests for up to an hour between each mating and will strike any tom that approaches before she is ready.

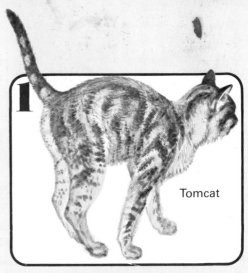

1

Tomcat

Some toms will court and mate only in their own territory, which they mark out by spraying with their urine (see page 8). When a tom finds a female on heat, his first move is to spray the area with urine.

2

Female rejects tom by growling and striking at him with her claws out.

Tomcat

When a female is on heat, she calls to attract toms to her and gives off a smell which they find very attractive. For two to three days, the toms court her, but she is not ready to mate and will reject advances made by any of them. This is a safeguard from the wild, to give the males plenty of time to find the female before she goes off heat.

3

Female crouches with her rear up and her tail held to one side.

When she is ready to mate, the female's mood changes. She begins to roll and rubs her head against anything nearby. She then crouches low, making treading movements with her hind legs and purring.

4

Tomcat grasps female by scruff of neck.

When he sees that the female is ready, the tom approaches her sideways from behind. He mounts her, grasping the scruff of her neck with his teeth and gripping her body between his front legs. The female remains still while the tom thrusts his penis into her, releasing his sperm. After a few seconds, she lets out a piercing cry and pulls away from him by twisting sideways.

5

Immediately after mating, the female rolls over and over and licks herself frantically. If the tom tries to approach again at this time, the female will growl and strike out at him.

How an unborn kitten grows

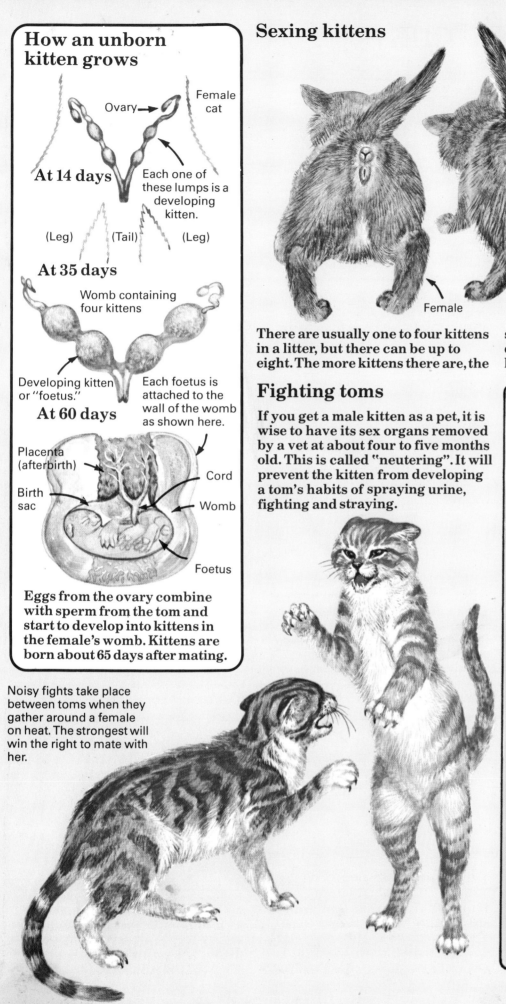

Ovary → Female cat

At 14 days

Each one of these lumps is a developing kitten.

(Leg) (Tail) (Leg)

At 35 days

Womb containing four kittens

Developing kitten or "foetus."

Each foetus is attached to the wall of the womb as shown here.

At 60 days

Placenta (afterbirth)

Birth sac

Cord

Womb

Foetus

Eggs from the ovary combine with sperm from the tom and start to develop into kittens in the female's womb. Kittens are born about 65 days after mating.

Noisy fights take place between toms when they gather around a female on heat. The strongest will win the right to mate with her.

Sexing kittens

To tell whether a kitten is male or female, lift up its tail and look closely at its rear. If the two small back openings are about twelve millimetres apart, the kitten is a male. If they are very close together and appear to meet, the kitten is a female.

Female

Male (about 4 weeks old)

There are usually one to four kittens in a litter, but there can be up to eight. The more kittens there are, the smaller they will be. It is quite difficult to tell male and female kittens apart.

Fighting toms

If you get a male kitten as a pet, it is wise to have its sex organs removed by a vet at about four to five months old. This is called "neutering". It will prevent the kitten from developing a tom's habits of spraying urine, fighting and straying.

How many kittens?

FEMALE CAT

= ONE LITTER (4 KITTENS AVERAGE)

AT 3 YEARS
+
AT 5 YEARS
+
AT 7 YEARS
+
AT 9 YEARS
+
AT 11 YEARS

= 100 KITTENS

A female cat is able to mate again within a few weeks of giving birth. She can produce as many as 100 kittens during her life as this chart shows. If you get a female kitten as a pet, it may be best to have her sex organs removed by a vet so she cannot have kittens. This is called "spaying."

The birth of kittens

During the last week of her pregnancy, a female cat becomes less active. Her stomach is very large and her nipples are pink and swollen. Cats are naturally excellent mothers. They rarely need help with the birth of their kittens unless there are any complications. The kittens are usually born not more than one hour apart, and a whole litter may be produced in less than an hour.

After the birth of the last kitten, the mother cleans her hindquarters and then curls herself round on her side so that she encircles and protects the kittens while they suckle. As long as she continues to feed the kittens, the mother is likely to lose weight even though she will eat more. She should be given two or three times as much food as normal.

The first three weeks of a kitten's life are roughly equal to the first 18 months of a human baby's life. The kittens do not venture out of the nest until they start to walk at about three weeks old. They may pat one another and begin to play by the end of the third week.

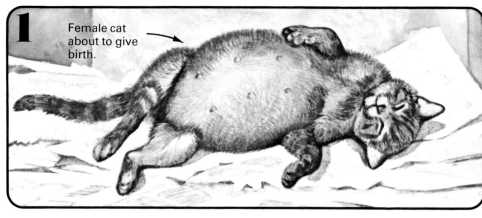

1 Female cat about to give birth.

If your cat is going to have kittens, you should provide her with a strong cardboard box lined with clean newspaper. The box should be put in a warm, quiet, draught-free place where the cat will not be disturbed. When she is about to give birth, the cat will become restless and she may begin shredding the paper in her box to make a nest.

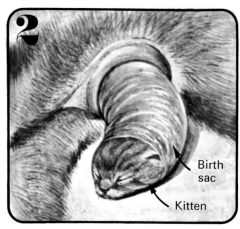

2 Birth sac. Kitten

Each kitten is born in a thin, transparent bag or sac. This sac breaks either at birth or just before, releasing the fluid inside it.

3 Newborn kitten

The mother cat bites the cord, licks the newly born kitten vigorously to get it breathing and to dry it, then eats the afterbirth.

4 Kitten suckles from mother's teat.

Hold kitten in one hand like this. Newborn kittens must be fed every two hours.

Control milk flow by holding finger over open end of bottle.

As soon as a kitten has been dried, it searches for a teat to suckle from. Kittens are born blind, so they find their mother's teats by smell and touch.

If a cat has more than four kittens, she may not be able to feed them all. You can feed young kittens using a special feeding bottle like this. A cat's milk is much richer than cow's milk, so ask your vet how to make up a substitute feed. If a kitten is fed on cow's milk alone, it will starve to death. The vet will also tell you how often to feed kittens as they get older.

5 One week old

The mother washes each kitten, especially around its head and tail. Washing around its tail makes the kitten excrete. The mother eats the urine and solid waste to keep the nest clean.

By the time the kittens are a week old, each one in the litter will have "claimed" a teat as its own. It will now feed only from this teat.

For the first one or two days after birth, the mother stays with her kittens continuously. After they are about a week old, she will leave them for several hours at a time. The kittens keep warm when she is away by sleeping in a heap, but as soon as she comes back they nuzzle up to her and start feeding. The kittens can only crawl along on their stomachs at this stage and spend most of their time suckling and sleeping. They grow quickly and double their weight in the first nine days.

Kitten is born blind. Its eyes stay closed for about nine days.

Kitten's claws are not yet retractable.

Kitten has no teeth for the first two weeks.

If a kitten gets separated from its mother it lets out a shrill wailing sound which enables its mother to find it.

6 Nine days old

Eyes just opening.

At about nine days old, the kittens' eyes open. All kittens' eyes are a milky blue colour when they first open. It is a few days before the kitten can see properly.

7 Three weeks old

By three weeks old, the kittens can stand quite well and they take their first steps. Hearing improves and their baby or "milk" teeth are beginning to appear.

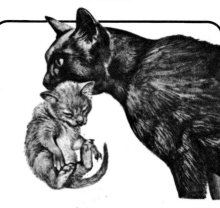

If a mother cat senses danger she will carry her kittens to safety. She picks each one up in her mouth by the scruff of its neck. The kitten curls up into a ball to protect itself.

Growing up

Between four to eight weeks is a very important time in a kitten's life. The experiences it has at this age shape its development as an adult, so it should have plenty of contact with people during this period.

At three to four weeks, the mother leaves the kittens on their own for longer, but she is still very protective towards them. Kittens begin to eat some solid food at about four weeks, so they take less milk. (This process is called "weaning"). By the time they are six to eight weeks old, kittens are quite independent.

A mother's ability to produce milk depends on the kittens continuing to suckle. Kittens develop a kneading action with their forepaws to encourage the flow of milk.

As kittens grow stronger they play more vigorously. They tire easily at this stage and fall asleep in a pile so that they keep each other warm.

Coming out of the nest

The mother continues to groom her kittens until they are about seven weeks old. As they grow up, they often respond by licking her face and neck.

Kittens paw at each other's faces and bodies when they first start to play together. Playing is very important, as it helps them to develop skills they will need as adults.

Kittens' sense of smell is well developed. They sniff at everything around them.

By four weeks old, the kittens are exploring their surroundings thoroughly. They will have most of their milk teeth and will bite and chew everything they find. As they spend more time out of the nest, they will start to excrete away from it. It is useful to keep a bucket of water and sponge handy for mopping up.

Kittens use their paws to investigate things that interest them. They hook objects towards them for closer inspection. By four weeks their claws have become retractable.

Weaning

1

When kittens leave the nest, they will see their mother eating from a bowl, and may try imitating her. You can begin weaning kittens now with baby food or dried milk, made up as indicated on the packet.

2

Kittens should be introduced to solid food, such as finely minced raw meat, in the fourth week when they have most of their milk teeth. They should have learned to lap and chew, and be fully weaned by the time they are six weeks old.

Cat litter or earth in tray.

When it moves from the nest a kitten may imitate its mother and use a toilet tray. If it is slow to learn, you can help by placing it on a tray regularly after meals.

Learning from mother

1

By the time they are six weeks old, kittens have become very adventurous and will play with almost anything. The mother cat is very tolerant and will allow them to play with her tail, twitching it invitingly to and fro. The kittens start to learn hunting skills by stalking and pouncing on her tail.

2

The mother cat actively encourages her kittens to play, but if they become too rough or misbehave, she will bat them with her paw.

3

Kittens have to be taught to recognize danger. They have little sense of fear and must learn from their mother which animals are friends or enemies.

4

Kittens learn how to groom and wash themselves by watching and imitating their mother. They often groom one another.

Handling kittens

Mother will watch anxiously when you pick up a kitten.

From six weeks old, kittens should be handled frequently so that they get used to being picked up and will not scratch and bite. Always pick up a kitten or cat with one hand underneath to support it.

A new pet

Many people find kittens irresistible and are tempted to buy one on impulse. But a kitten soon grows into a cat and most cats live to at least ten years of age. Although cats are very independent animals, they need affection and companionship, so do not get one if you are likely to be away from home a lot.

There are many lovely breeds of cats (see pages 30 and 31), but most people prefer a mongrel (a cross-bred cat). Pure bred cats cost a lot of money and are usually kept by people for entering in shows.

Points to look for

Clean ears, no brown specks inside.

Clean nose, not runny.

Bright eyes.

Full set of teeth.

Glossy coat.

Clean and dry underneath tail.

Sturdy body and limbs.

You can buy kittens from pet shops, but if possible, buy one from the house where it has been born so that you can see that the mother cat is alert, healthy and well cared for.

Kittens should not be taken from their mother until they are fully weaned at about seven or eight weeks. When you go to collect your kitten take a cat-carrying basket with you. Ask whether the kitten has been vaccinated against feline infectious enteritis. If not, you should take it to a vet straight away as this disease can kill cats.

Cardboard or wooden box with hole cut in one side makes a good bed. Line with newspaper and an old rug. If very cold, add a hot-water bottle (hand-hot water) wrapped in a blanket.

Plastic tray with sides about 8 cm high. Half-fill with cat litter and place on newspaper in a quiet corner. Change litter frequently.

If your kitten is likely to spend a lot of time outside when older, you should get it used to wearing a collar with an address tag. The collar should have an elastic insert so that the cat will not get strangled if caught while climbing a tree.

Elastic

Fresh water

Kitten should start with four small meals of varied food a day.

Cotton reel

Ball of silver paper.

Ping-pong ball

Bell tied onto twig.

Kitten can be kept amused with simple toys such as these.

Before you take a new kitten home, you should get a few things ready. The most essential is a warm bed. A cardboard or wooden box is best, with newspaper and an old rug for bedding. Put the box in a corner away from draughts and where there is not too much noise.

The kitten should have fresh water available at all times and a litter tray. Even if you have a garden and plan to let the kitten excrete outside, you should provide it with a litter tray for a few weeks, until it knows you and is used to its new home.

Keep the kitten in one room to start with and gradually introduce it to the rest of the home over the next few days. Let it run around and explore its surroundings, and do not handle it too much at first. The breeder or pet shop will give you instructions for feeding.

1 Training

Cat flap

If you have a garden, you can train your kitten to ask to go outside to excrete. A cat flap fitted in the door allows a cat to come and go as it pleases.

2

Cats can be trained to claw at special scratching posts rather than at furniture. Hold the cat up to the post and move its paws up and down. You can buy posts at pet shops.

3

DON'T ALLOW KITTEN ON WORK SURFACES. IT IS UNHYGIENIC.

DON'T ALLOW KITTEN NEAR ELECTRIC FLEXES. IT MIGHT GET A SHOCK IF IT CHEWS A PLUGGED-IN FLEX.

DON'T ALLOW KITTEN ON TOP OF COOKER OR HIGH LEVEL GRILL. KITTENS LOVE WARMTH BUT THEY COULD EASILY BURN THEMSELVES.

Kittens are very inquisitive, so care must be taken to keep them away from dangers in the home, especially in the kitchen.

Do not allow a kitten to play near anyone who is cooking, in case they trip over it. Always guard fireplaces and electric fires.

Exercise

You should play with your kitten as often as possible to exercise it and prevent it from becoming bored. All kittens love to chase and pounce on small objects tied to string.

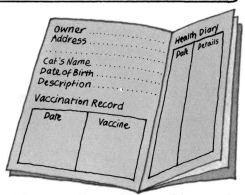

When you first take your kitten to be vaccinated, the vet will give you a certificate which shows when booster jabs will be needed. The certificate may be like this one, with space for notes about your cat's health. Make your own record book if you are not given one.

Make a catnip mouse

Catnip or catmint plants have a smell that is attractive to most cats. It makes them rub and roll in pleasure. You can make your cat a toy using material or felt scraps and dried catnip leaves.

Pick several sprigs of catnip and hang it up to dry.

1 What you need

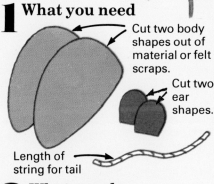

Cut two body shapes out of material or felt scraps.

Cut two ear shapes.

Length of string for tail

2 What you do

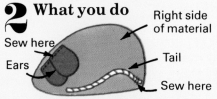

Right side of material

Sew here

Ears

Tail

Sew here

Lay ears and tail on right side of one body shape and sew into place.

3

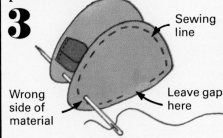

Sewing line

Wrong side of material

Leave gap here

Put second body shape on top of first (right sides of material together) and sew together, leaving gap for turning mouse right side out.

4

Eye

Turn mouse right side out. Stuff with dried catnip and sew up hole in body. Draw on eyes with a marking pen.

Looking after your cat

Cats make excellent pets. They are very easy to look after, as they do not need long walks or much training. A cat's main requirements for a healthy and happy life are the correct diet, cleanliness, warmth and human company. Feeding time is the high spot in a cat's day, so feed your cat at the same time each day as far as possible. Feed food at room temperature and do not leave uneaten food lying around.

From the time it is weaned, a kitten should be encouraged to eat a variety of foods. Cats can be very fussy eaters and if allowed to develop preferences may not eat a balanced diet. Adult cats need only one meal a day, but many people prefer to feed two slightly smaller meals. An adult male cat should weigh about 4½ kilograms and a female about 3 kilograms. Weigh your cat occasionally to make sure you are not overfeeding it.

Cats are very healthy animals. They do not need an annual check-up, but if you have any worries about your cat's health, do take it to a vet. Beware of taking in stray cats as they are often unhealthy and may have roundworms or tapeworms.

Dried food (always give the cat water with dried food).

Canned meat

Fresh water   Milk

Water 70%   Fat 10%
Carbohydrate 1%
Protein 14%   Minerals 1%

Cats can be fed raw foods, such as meat and offal, table scraps, fish, canned food, dried food or semi-dry food. Some also enjoy fresh milk but this may cause diarrhoea. Canned food is probably the best. It contains about 70 per cent water.

If you feed your cat dried food, you must make sure that it also has plenty of milk or water. A good idea is to mix the dried food with warm water. Eaten in large amounts, it can cause cats, especially neutered toms, severe problems in passing urine.

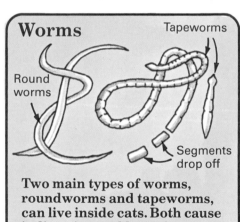

Mice are an ideal food for a cat. The circle shows what a mouse is made up of. It also contains vitamins in its liver.

Fleas and ear mites

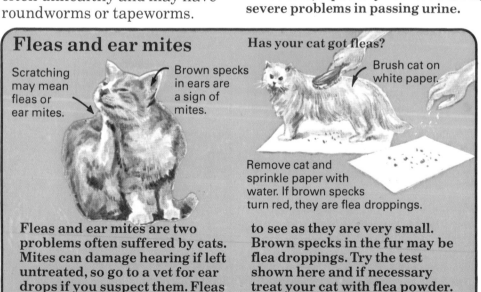

Scratching may mean fleas or ear mites.

Brown specks in ears are a sign of mites.

Has your cat got fleas?

Brush cat on white paper.

Remove cat and sprinkle paper with water. If brown specks turn red, they are flea droppings.

Fleas and ear mites are two problems often suffered by cats. Mites can damage hearing if left untreated, so go to a vet for ear drops if you suspect them. Fleas live in cats' fur and are difficult to see as they are very small. Brown specks in the fur may be flea droppings. Try the test shown here and if necessary treat your cat with flea powder. Follow the directions on the tin.

Worms

Tapeworms

Round worms

Segments drop off

Two main types of worms, roundworms and tapeworms, can live inside cats. Both cause indigestion and loss of condition. They are passed out in the cat's solid waste. Take your cat to a vet if you think it has worms.

Grooming

Use a bristle brush to groom your cat.

As soon as you get a kitten you should establish a grooming routine. Short-haired cats should be groomed once a week but long-haired ones need daily brushing. Any badly matted fur must be gently cut off.

Travel

If you have to take your cat on journeys or to the vet, it is advisable to carry it in a special basket with a secure fastening. Line the bottom of the basket with paper to keep out draughts.

Illness and injury

The most common sign of illness in cats is loss of appetite combined with vomiting. Never attempt to treat a cat yourself, always go to a vet.

If your cat is ill with a temperature or vomiting, wrap it up warmly and put it in a darkened room. A sick cat may bite, so handle it as little as possible. Call the vet.

If a cat gets run over, lay it on newspaper in a cardboard box, cover to keep warm and take it to a vet immediately.

Holidays

Warm, clean sleeping quarters

Clean bedding

Scratching post

Individual wired run

Fresh water

Food

If you go away, whether for a weekend or a long holiday, you must arrange for your cat to be looked after. Either ask a reliable neighbour to come in and feed the cat at its normal meal times or, for longer holidays, find recognized cat boarding kennels. Always go and look at kennels before you book to make sure they are clean and well equipped and that any cats there are being well cared for. You will need to book well in advance, especially in the summer.

DO'S AND DON'TS

DON'T LET A CAT EAT FROM DISHES THAT YOU USE YOURSELF. IT MAY BE CARRYING GERMS IN ITS MOUTH.

DON'T HANDLE A CAT TOO MUCH OR KISS OR NUZZLE IT. IT MAY SCRATCH YOU IF IT IS FEELING FED UP.

DON'T LET A CAT SLEEP ON YOUR BED. IT MAY HAVE FLEAS.

DON'T PUT A CAT OUT AT NIGHT. IT MAY CHOOSE TO GO OUT IF IT HAS A CAT FLAP, BUT DON'T FORCE IT TO.

DO WASH A CAT'S DISHES SEPARATELY, USING HOT SOAPY WATER. WASH THEM IMMEDIATELY AFTER EACH MEAL.

DO WASH YOUR HANDS AFTER HANDLING A CAT. CATS ARE VERY CLEAN ANIMALS BUT THEY CAN CARRY GERMS.

DO PROVIDE A CAT WITH ITS OWN BED AND PUT IT IN A WARM PLACE AWAY FROM DRAUGHTS.

Kinds of cats

Domestic cats are divided into groups based on features such as shape of head and fur length. The grouping and naming of cats differs slightly in different countries but two main groups, longhair and shorthair cats, are recognized everywhere. Shorthair cats are divided into two groups: British or American and Foreign shorthairs.

Groups, or breeds, of cats are divided even further according to the colour and pattern of their coats and their eye colour. For example, the tabby is a British shorthair with distinctive coat markings. There are three kinds, or varieties, of tabby: brown, red and silver.

Words used for describing cats
Cobby: sturdily built body.
Ear tufts: tufts of hair at base of ears.
Mask: the face.
Persian: any longhair cat.
Points: feet, legs, ears, tail and mask. Most commonly used in describing Siamese cats, which have points of a different colour from main coat colour.
Ruff: the fur around the neck.
Self: a cat whose coat is the same colour all over, with no markings.
Ticked: hairs whose tips are a different colour from the rest of the hair.
Whisker pads: muscular pads from which the whiskers sprout.

Foreign shorthair

Seal-pointed Siamese

Foreign shorthairs have short coats and are slim and dainty. They have long, wedge-shaped heads, large, pointed ears and slanting eyes.

British or American shorthair

Brown tabby

British or American shorthairs have medium length coats and stocky bodies. They have broad heads with fairly short ears and noses.

Longhair

Blue persian

Longhaired cats have long, glossy fur and cobby bodies. They have short legs and a broad head with small ears and a very short nose.

Semi-longhair

Birman

Semi-longhaired cats are grouped with longhaired cats but they have a shorter coat. There are two varieties, Birman and Turkish.

Breeding

From time to time, cats give birth to kittens that differ slightly in appearance from all the existing varieties of cats. If such a kitten is admired, it will be carefully selected and bred with another similar-looking cat. In this way, a new variety of cat gradually emerges. All the many different kinds of pedigree, or pure bred, cats that exist today are the result of this selective kind of breeding.

A pedigree cat is one whose family tree is known for at least five generations. Its pedigree must be officially registered.

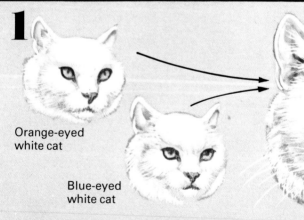

Orange-eyed white cat

Blue-eyed white cat

Odd-eyed white cat

White cats with blue eyes tend to be deaf. To correct this fault, breeders sometimes cross them with orange-eyed whites. Quite often one of the kittens in the resulting litter will have one eye which is deep blue and the other which is a bright orange.

How to make a cat survey

You can find out which kinds of cats are the most common in your neighbourhood by making your own survey. With the help of a street map, draw a plan of the area in which you live, marking in houses, roads and paths.

Walk around the area and look for cats at least once every day for a week. Mark on your map where you see each cat, using a different colour dot for each different kind of cat. Try to remember the cats you see so that you mark each cat down on your map once only.

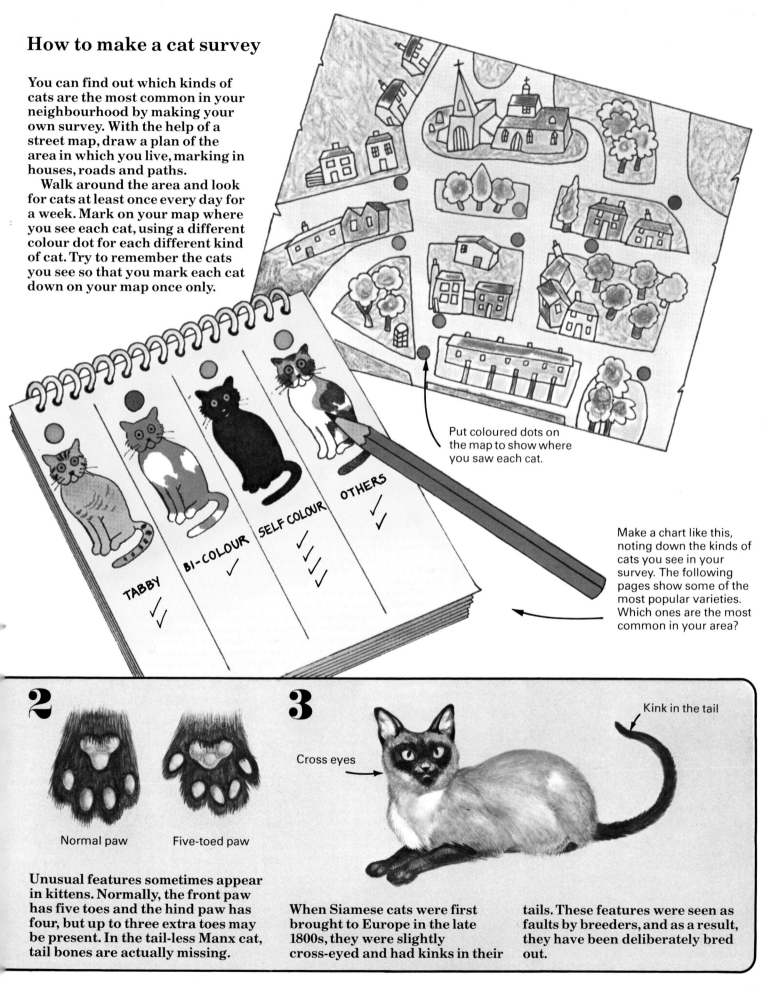

Put coloured dots on the map to show where you saw each cat.

TABBY

BI-COLOUR

SELF COLOUR

OTHERS

Make a chart like this, noting down the kinds of cats you see in your survey. The following pages show some of the most popular varieties. Which ones are the most common in your area?

2

Normal paw   Five-toed paw

Unusual features sometimes appear in kittens. Normally, the front paw has five toes and the hind paw has four, but up to three extra toes may be present. In the tail-less Manx cat, tail bones are actually missing.

3

Cross eyes

Kink in the tail

When Siamese cats were first brought to Europe in the late 1800s, they were slightly cross-eyed and had kinks in their tails. These features were seen as faults by breeders, and as a result, they have been deliberately bred out.

Cats to look for: Shorthairs

Red and white

Devon Rex

Abyssinian

Black and white

Cornish Rex

Red Abyssinian

Bi-coloured. Coat is one plain colour and white, but not more than two-thirds of it should be coloured. Chest, chin, belly and front legs are usually white. Eyes are orange, copper or yellow.

Russian Blue. Grey-blue coat is thick and silky. Notice the large whisker pads. Bright-green, almond shaped eyes. A quiet voice.

Cornish Rex. Very short wavy coat with no guard hairs. Can be any colour. Whiskers are crinkled and broken. There is also a Devon Rex with the same coat, but larger eyes and very large ears.

Abyssinian. Coat is rabbit coloured all over (no stripes), each hair being ruddy brown with bands of black or brown. Almond shaped eyes. There is also a Red Abyssinian.

Tabby-pointed Siamese

Seal-pointed Siamese

Tortoiseshell and white. Also called Calico. Distinct black and red patches on a white background. Orange, copper or hazel eyes.

Manx. Easily recognized because it has no tail. Coat can be any colour or pattern. Hindquarters are very high and hind legs are long.

Brown Burmese. Rich, dark seal-brown glossy coat, lighter on the chest and belly. Ears and mask may be slightly darker. Slanting yellow eyes.

Siamese. Cream or white coat with some darker shading, the colour of which depends on the colour of the points. Points can be seal, chocolate, blue, red, lilac, tabby or tortie (tortoiseshell). Eyes are clear blue in all varieties. Siamese cats have points because colour develops only in the cooler parts of the body: the ears, face, tail and limbs.

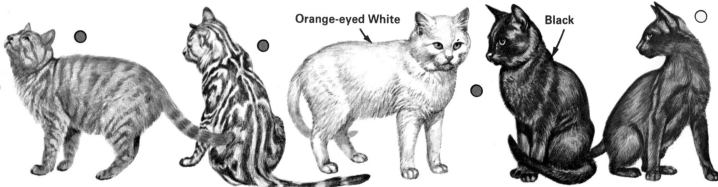

Orange-eyed White

Black

Red Tabby. Deep orange coat (not ginger) with distinct tabby markings of a darker red colour. There should not be any white. Hazel or orange eyes. Red tabbies are usually males. There is also a brown tabby shorthair.

Silver Tabby. Pure silver-grey coat with black tabby markings. These can be narrow (called mackerel) or wide (blotched). Green or hazel eyes.

Orange-eyed White. Pure white coat and deep orange or copper eyes. There are also blue-eyed and odd-eyed white shorthairs. **Black.** Another variety of self-coloured cat. Coat is jet black and eyes are deep orange or copper.
  There are two other self-coloured shorthairs, one is called Blue and the other Cream.

Havana. Rich dark brown coat with no markings. Whiskers, nose and mouth are also brown. Large ears and a long tail. Green eyes.

● **British or American shorthairs** ○ **Foreign shorthairs**

Longhairs

The cats shown here are pedigree cats. Most of the cats you will see in your neighbourhood will probably be cross-bred or mongrel cats, but many of them may look similar to those shown here. The best place to see pedigree cats is a cat show.

Seal Colourpoint

Colourpoint. Cream or white coat with points like a Siamese, but the long hair and body shape of a Persian. The points can be different colours as with the Siamese. Blue eyes.

Cream. Long, silky, pure cream coloured coat, with short bushy tail and small tufted ears. Short thick legs. Large, round, deep copper coloured eyes.

Brown Tabby. Brown coat with black tabby markings. M-mark on forehead and bands around the legs and tail. Hazel or copper eyes. There are also red and silver longhaired tabbies.

Turkish. A semi-longhaired cat. Coat is chalk white with ginger markings on face and a ginger tail. Large upright ears. Amber coloured eyes. It is an unusual cat as it loves being in water.

Black. Pure black coat. Orange or copper eyes. Kittens may have a rusty black coat but as they get older, it changes to pure black. If a cat spends a lot of time in the sun, the coat may develop a brownish tinge.

Smoke. Silver neck ruff around a black face, with silver ear tufts. White undercoat. Top-coat is black on the back, shading to silver-grey on the sides of the body. Legs are black. Orange or copper eyes.

Red Self. You will not often see a cat with the correct coat colouring. It should be deep orange without tabby markings. Deep copper eyes.

Chinchilla. Undercoat is white, but each hair is tipped with black so the coat looks silver-grey. Skin on paw-pads and around eyelids is black. Eyes are emerald or blue-green.

Black and white

Cream and white

Orange-eyed White. Pure white coat with no shading or marking of any kind. Brilliant orange or copper eyes. There are also blue-eyed and odd-eyed white longhaired cats.

Seal-pointed Birman. A semi-longhaired cat with creamy-brown coat and seal points. Easily recognised by the pure white socks on its feet. China blue eyes.

Bi-coloured. One plain colour and white, with not more than two-thirds of coat being coloured. Chin, chest, front legs and shoulders are white. Copper or orange eyes.

Tortoiseshell. Coat of black, red and cream in patches. Almost always females. Males are rare and are usually unable to mate successfully. Orange or copper eyes.

Sacred and mythical cats

Bast

An Egyptian statue of a cat, sacred to the goddess Bast.

A picture from an Egyptian papyrus

The serpent of darkness

Bast

In ancient Egypt, the cat was sacred to the cat goddess Bast. The Egyptians believed that she was the sun-eye and the moon-eye of their sky god.

As the moon-eye, Bast could see in the dark. Every night she was supposed to battle with the serpent of darkness so that the sun could rise again the next day.

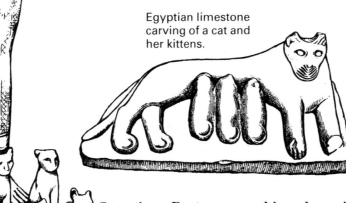

Egyptian limestone carving of a cat and her kittens.

"M" mark

Sometimes Bast was worshipped as a mother goddess. Young wives often wore necklaces, strung with a certain number of kitten charms. They would then pray to Bast for the same number of children.

The Egyptian name for a cat was "miw." Egyptian cats had the mark of an "M" on their fore-heads. Modern tabby cats with an M-mark may be related to the ancient miws.

The Siamese cat

All Siamese cats have a shadowy patch on the back of their necks, sometimes called the "hand mark." There is one legend from Siam which tells how a god once picked up a sacred Siamese cat. Where his hand touched the animal, a shadowy mark was left. Ever since then, so the legend tells, all Siamese cats have been born with the same mark.

The "hand mark"

Mummified cat

All cats in ancient Egypt were sacred. When a cat died, it was embalmed and put in a mummy case. Its owners would shave off their eyebrows as a sign of mourning. Temple cats had special and very expensive funerals.

Phantom cats

Old tales of black phantom cats come from all over the world. Cat phantoms were usually evil, and if one sat on your bed it was a sure sign that you were about to die.

Witches

In the Middle Ages the cat was associated with the devil (another name for the devil was "old scratch"). Superstitions told of witches having cat "familiars." These were spirits provided by the devil to help them with their magic.

Witches were able to take the form of a cat nine times. There is an old record from a German witch trial that tells how one witch, who was being burned at the stake, escaped from the flames by changing herself into a cat.

Lucky cats

A Japanese Beckoning cat charm

In Japan, wearing a Beckoning cat charm is believed to bring you good luck. The original Beckoning cat comes from a legend. This describes how ancient Japanese warriors were once saved from a terrible storm by a little black cat who beckoned them into the safety of a temple. Japanese children often wear Beckoning cat toy necklaces.

Cat vampires

Japanese cat vampires disguised themselves as humans, but when they attacked their victims they would change into a two-tailed cat.

The Peruvian cat god

Old Peruvian pot showing the head of the cat god.

In ancient Peru the fertility god was an old cat-man. He had long fangs and cat whiskers.

Cats and the weather

There is a story that in ancient China, there was a winking cat which would wink when a storm was approaching.

In Sumatra they once believed that cats could control the weather. They would call up black rain clouds by throwing a black cat into the river.

Border Collie

German Shepherd Dog

Saluki

Part 2 written by
Su Swallow

Part 2 DOGS

This section begins by taking a look at the first tame dogs and their probable ancestor, the wolf. It goes on to show how dogs have been trained to work with man in many different roles, ranging from herding sheep and guarding buildings to guiding blind people.

Dogs' behaviour is described and explained in detail on pages 44-53. The different kinds of play and aggression, courtship behaviour and the development of puppies are all looked at. You can learn how to read dogs' language and discover for yourself the meaning behind their actions and expressions.

You can find out how to choose and care for a dog of your own on pages 54-55 and 58-60. Page 61 gives some advice on what to do if your dog is ill.

Whether you have a mongrel or a pedigree dog, its training is very important. Pages 56 and 57 will help you with basic training. Most towns have dog-training classes and if you are finding it difficult to train on your own, or if you would like to do some more advanced training, it might be a good idea to take your dog along. You will get expert advice and your dog will get used to being with other dogs.

The chart on pages 62-63 shows lots of common breeds of dogs to spot. All the different breeds have their own clubs or associations and most of these have a junior membership. For a small fee you will receive their newsletter. If you want to show your dog, many clubs have dog shows which have children's classes. The club secretary will probably be able to help you with questions you may have about your particular breed.

English Foxhound

From wolf to dog

The dog belongs to a group of animals known as the Canis family, which includes foxes, jackals and wolves. It is now thought that the dog is descended from the wolf, not only because of a likeness between their builds and behaviour, but because their bone structures are very similar. Mating between breeds of wolves probably gave rise to the first breeds of dogs.

Dogs were the first domesticated animals, and people began to use them for working about 10,000 years ago.

The wolf

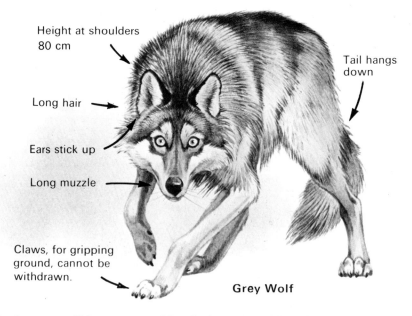

Height at shoulders 80 cm

Long hair

Ears stick up

Long muzzle

Claws, for gripping ground, cannot be withdrawn.

Tail hangs down

Grey Wolf

The wolf is the largest wild member of the Canis family. Wolves still survive in forests and mountains in Europe, Asia and North America. They live and hunt in packs, and each pack has a feeding territory or area. Some dogs still look like the wolf.

The first tame dogs

1 As pets

Thousands of years ago in the Stone Age, people went hunting for meat. They would have been followed by wolf packs and may have adopted abandoned wolf cubs as pets for their children.

2 As hunters

Breeding between these pet wolves produced the first dogs. Over many years, and perhaps by accident, people found that dogs could be useful on hunting trips.

3 As guard dogs

As people developed better tools they grew crops and kept herds of animals for food. Now the dogs could be useful in other ways, guarding the herds from wolves, as well as protecting the family.

Early breeds

Ancient wall carvings and statues of dogs have been found all over the world. Above is a scene from an old Egyptian tomb showing hounds, rather like modern Ibizan hounds, chasing ostriches. These hunting dogs could run fast over long distances and hunted by sight as well as by scent. Many breeds of tracking dogs, guard dogs and large, fierce battle-dogs, are also shown in ancient art.

Small pet watch dogs called "Lion Dogs" were kept by royalty in Ancient China. They were the ancestors of modern Pekingese dogs. These Ancient Chinese ornaments represent the Lion Dogs.

Working dogs

Alaskan Malamute

Originally, nearly all dogs were bred for working and today a few breeds, like these sledge dogs, are still kept strictly as working animals. People generally call sledge dogs

Huskies, but in fact there are many different breeds. They are all strong dogs that can pull heavy loads over long distances, with little food or rest. Their thick coats keep out the cold.

The Eskimos train their dog teams carefully. Each team will have a leader dog. Old dogs are not kept as pets but are killed and eaten, and their fur used for clothing.

Sporting dogs

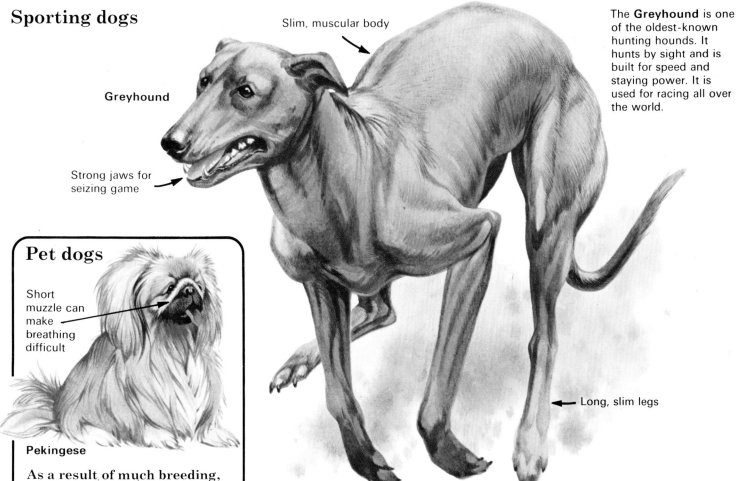

Slim, muscular body

Greyhound

Strong jaws for seizing game

The **Greyhound** is one of the oldest-known hunting hounds. It hunts by sight and is built for speed and staying power. It is used for racing all over the world.

Long, slim legs

Pet dogs

Short muzzle can make breathing difficult

Pekingese

As a result of much breeding, there are many different kinds of small or "toy" dogs. They make good pets because they need less food and exercise than large breeds. However, toy dogs with flat faces often have breathing problems.

There are many breeds of sporting dogs. Some, like the Greyhound, are used for racing, others for hunting. Each particular breed has been developed for the qualities needed for its sport. These range from speed and staying power, to a highly developed sense of sight or smell.

Many sporting dogs make good pets, but they usually need a lot of exercise.

Sporting dogs: hounds, terriers....

Hunting has led to the breeding of many well-known types of dog. Hunting dogs fall into three main groups: hounds, gundogs and terriers.

Dogs that both hunt and kill their game (deer, foxes and hares) are known as hounds. Hounds may work alone or in packs. Some breeds work silently while others bark.

Gundogs are also used to find game (often birds), but unlike hounds they do not kill it.

Terriers are usually small dogs, originally bred to follow animals down burrows or holes.

Hounds

Pack of **Beagles**

Hare

Most pack hounds work with hunters on horseback. They cover great distances, so they must be kept very fit (Foxhounds may travel 100 km a day to hunt foxes). Beagles, which hunt hares, are slower, so the hunt members can keep up with them on foot.

Pack hound puppies are usually looked after in pairs by a family ("puppy walkers"). They are given basic training and taught not to disturb any farm animals. Discipline is very important as they must learn to obey the huntsman. Later they learn to hunt by working with the older hounds.

Digging

Dachshund
(Smooth-haired)

Like other hounds, the Dachshund has a good sense of smell, and it can track and even retrieve game. It has strong front legs for digging into fox and rabbit holes.

Terriers

Staffordshire
Bull Terrier

Airedale
Terrier

Fox Terrier (Wire)

Terriers were bred originally to kill animal pests such as rats and foxes. They could hunt both above and below ground. Many were also used in the old sports of bull- and bear-baiting and for dog fights. Today, a few terriers are still used to hunt foxes and rabbits, but most are just kept as pets.

....and gundogs

Pointers and Setters

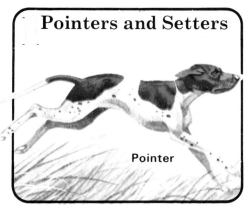

Pointer

A Pointer or Setter will race across country well ahead of its owner to find game, often grouse or partridge. It holds its head high, with nostrils open wide, to catch any scent of a bird.

2

As soon as it smells a bird, the dog will stop and stand completely still, its head pointing out the bird's position. This is called a "point". It waits in this position until its owner catches up.

3

The dog creeps forward to make the bird fly up. When a shot is fired, the dog drops to the ground and waits until ordered to move again. Pointers and Setters are not usually trained to retrieve.

Retrievers and Spaniels

Labrador Retriever

Retrievers and Spaniels are used for flushing or frightening out game birds and animals (such as pheasants, ducks and rabbits) and for retrieving shot game. They will even retrieve game that has fallen

2

Golden Retriever

into water. Some have thick coats which help prevent them getting badly scratched while they are working in thick undergrowth. They are taught not to be distracted by other animals.

3

English Springer Spaniel

A dog that retrieves must carry the game gently in its mouth so as not to damage it. It should run straight back to its owner, without dropping the game, and deliver it into his hand.

Training a gundog

When a gundog has been trained in basic obedience, it is taught not to be frightened by the sound of a gun. In one exercise, shots are fired up into the air at a distance. The dog is taught to drop at a hand signal or whistle blast, given when the gun is fired. Eventually, the dog learns to drop when it hears the gunshot.

All-purpose dogs

Weimaraner

Some dogs, like this German Weimaraner, are bred and trained to point, to flush out game and to retrieve.

Working dogs

Dogs have been bred as working animals all over the world for thousands of years. Most were used to herd and guard livestock, and these are still the most common jobs for working dogs today. In the past, many breeds were used to pull milk floats, bakers' carts and other loads, and today, in some countries, people still use dogs to pull sledges.

Many working breeds, including sheepdogs, are also popular as pet and show dogs. In some countries, working dogs in shows are judged on their ability to work, as well as on their appearance.

In sheepdog trials, the dog has to herd a few sheep in the same way that he would herd a large flock on the farm. The dog must work closely with the shepherd, obeying whistle and voice commands. These tell him to move, stay still or go to the left or right of the flock.

Sheepdogs often have to work on their own, especially in hilly or mountainous country. Many countries have developed breeds to cope with their own kinds of landscape and climate.

Sheep dogs

1 Holding

Border Collie

A Border Collie can hold a group of sheep still by gazing steadily at them. The sheep sense the dog's attention and are afraid to move.

2 Driving

One of a sheepdog's most important jobs is to move flocks of sheep from one part of the farm to another, perhaps to a new grazing area, or for shearing or dipping.

The dog drives the sheep in front of it by running behind them. It keeps a large flock together by running to and fro at the back of the flock, and steers them to the left or right by running up the opposite side of the flock.

3 In the snow

In bad weather, the sheepdog rounds up the sheep so that they do not get lost. It can find sheep buried in snow drifts, and will dig, or point its head to indicate the spot.

4 Working in pairs

Sometimes shepherds need two or more dogs to control large flocks of sheep. The dogs learn to work together. Here, they are shedding, or separating the flock. One dog holds its sheep still, while the other drives its sheep away.

5 Backing

Red Kelpie

The Australian Kelpie is used to herd sheep in the same way as the Collie, but where the sheep are crowded together in a yard or pen, it runs over their backs and barks to keep them moving in the right direction. This is called "backing."

The Kelpie is descended from the Border Collie, but it has a shorter coat, better suited to the heat of Australia.

6 Guarding

Pyrenean Mountain Dog

Wolf

Guard dogs are usually larger than herding dogs. The massive Pyrenean Mountain Dog was used by the Romans as a guard dog. In Europe it was used to guard sheep against wolves and bears, and was often left alone for days at a time.

A cattle dog

Blue Heeler

The Australian cattle dog is known as the Blue Heeler because it nips cows on the heel to keep them moving.

A dog with many jobs

In the past, herding livestock and guarding were usually done by the same dog. A nomadic tribe in the Arctic still use Samoyeds as all-purpose dogs, for herding reindeer, hunting, guarding and pulling their sledges. However, in general herding and guarding are now done by different types of dogs.

Samoyed

Working dogs

Apart from herding and transport work, dogs have been bred to do many other jobs, most of which involve tracking, guarding or guide work.

A dog's sense of smell is very acute, which makes it an ideal animal for mountain rescue work. The police and army also use dogs for tracking work, and for sniffing out explosives.

In the two world wars, dogs were trained to sniff out land-mines or injured people. They were also used by army patrols in the jungle, to give early warning of an advancing enemy.

The German Shepherd Dog is used by the army for guarding and tracking. As part of its training, it is taught to jump over high walls.

Security firms often use German Shepherd Dogs as guard dogs. Training includes jumping through hoops of fire.

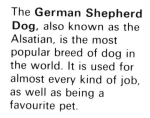

The **German Shepherd Dog,** also known as the Alsatian, is the most popular breed of dog in the world. It is used for almost every kind of job, as well as being a favourite pet.

This breed is used by police to track missing people. It is also used in mountain rescue work.

German Shepherd Dogs are one of the breeds used as guide dogs for the blind.

In Germany where the fields are often unfenced, it is used as a herding dog to prevent the sheep from straying.

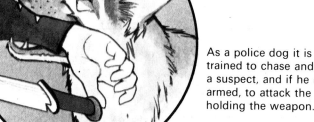

As a police dog it is trained to chase and hold a suspect, and if he is armed, to attack the arm holding the weapon.

Mountain rescue

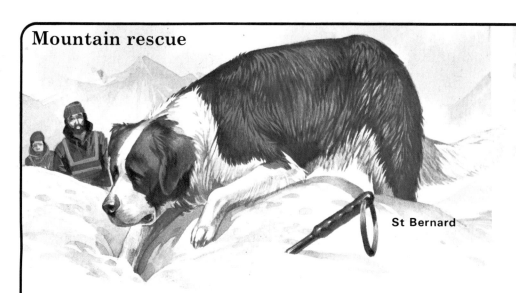

St Bernard

Dog searches by zig-zagging across snow.

Dogs are very useful for mountain rescue work. They can move over the snow faster than men, and can smell a person buried under several metres of snow. Mountain rescue dogs are owned by volunteers, who are called out when needed, often after heavy snowfalls or when there has been an avalanche.

During its training, the dog is sent to look for its trainer, who has buried himself in the snow. It is taught to dig only when it can smell that the person is alive.

Army dogs

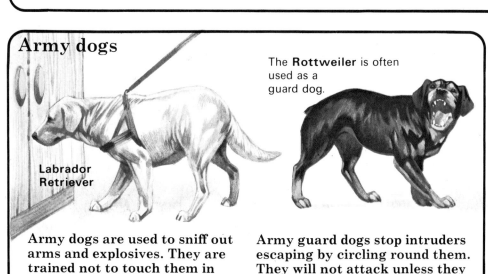

Labrador Retriever

The **Rottweiler** is often used as a guard dog.

Army dogs are used to sniff out arms and explosives. They are trained not to touch them in case they are booby-trapped.

Army guard dogs stop intruders escaping by circling round them. They will not attack unless they are attacked themselves.

Guide dogs

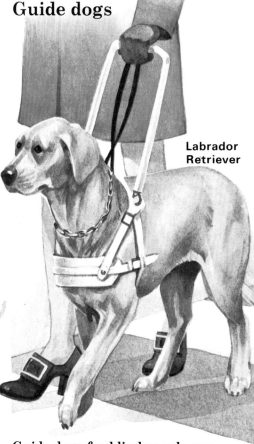

Labrador Retriever

Guide dogs for blind people are usually females, because they are easier to train than males, and not so easily distracted by other dogs.

Puppies are looked after by a family, usually in a town, so that they get used to noise, crowds and traffic. Later they are given several months' special training.

Guard dogs

Dobermann

Bullmastiff

Several large breeds such as the ones shown above, are used by the police, army and security firms as guard dogs. They must be very fit and are trained to chase and hold intruders. They usually learn to obey more than one handler.

43

Fighting and playing

The breed and sex of a dog both affect how friendly it is likely to be. Some Terriers, for example, can be very aggressive if strange dogs come too close, whereas Beagles, which work in packs and are therefore used to other dogs, do not usually mind strange dogs. Bitches (female dogs) tend to fight less and are usually submissive (will give way) to male dogs. However, a bitch with young pups can be very aggressive if the puppies are threatened.

Training can also affect a dog's behaviour. A well-trained dog will be obedient in most situations and so is less likely to become involved in a fight with another dog.

Most dogs will defend their home territory against unwanted visitors, especially other dogs of the same sex. This is called territorial aggression. The smallest dog may protect its home ground against the largest hound simply by looking threatening.

A dog chasing an animal shows hunting aggression. This is encouraged in police and army work.

Territorial fighting

1 The challenge

Tail up and stiff

Eyes staring into other dog's eyes

Ears are up

Hackles (fur) on neck and backbone are up

If two dogs meet in an area of land or territory that each regards as its own, such as a park, they may challenge each other as shown above. They both try to look threatening, by making themselves look as large and impressive as possible. To show off its size and strength each dog stands sideways-on to its rival. They then circle round, each trying to make the other dog give way.

Asking to play

If a dog starts to play in front of another dog or person with a play-object, it is usually trying to tempt them into joining in a game.

Playing

1 Hunting games

Dog pins down toy with its paws

Play pose

Games are a way of practising for real events. In hunting games a dog may stalk and chase its "prey", a toy or rag, before pinning it down.

Then the dog circles and leaps round its "prey", landing in a play pose. After "killing" it by chewing or pulling, the dog ignores the toy for a while, then starts again.

2 The fight

They will try to bite each other's throat, muzzle and ears.

Keeping a distance

Some dogs will attack if a strange dog or person comes too close. Just how close the stranger may come varies from dog to dog. Sometimes a dog may not be sure how to react when approached. Its face may look friendly, but its tail and hackles show that it might attack.

Usually the challenge ends with one of the dogs giving in to the threats of the other and turning away. If neither gives in, they may start to fight. The dogs push at each other's shoulders, growling and snapping, each trying to get its rival to the ground. If the fight becomes serious, they will attack each other's throat and muzzle.

3 Victory and defeat

The victor

Total submission pose (of the loser)

If one dog wants to admit defeat, it will roll over on to its back and expose its throat. This is a sign of giving in, because during the serious part of the fight the throat has been the main target for biting. At this signal, the other dog suddenly stops attacking. Unless the loser starts to become aggressive again, the winner slowly relaxes and allows the other dog, its tail down, to get up and leave.

If these two dogs meet again, the loser will remember that the other dog is superior. It will show its inferiority by turning side on to the other dog so that their bodies form a T shape. The other dog will not attack.

2 Pack games

Pack leader

Dogs often play in groups or packs, running after or chasing each other. There is always a social order, running down from the pack leader (the most superior dog) to the bottom or most inferior dog. Play fighting helps keep the social order in the pack, or between pairs of dogs, since the most superior dog will always win. They wrestle as in a proper fight, but there are no real attacks or serious biting unless one dog becomes aggressive.

45

Scent

Although a dog has only limited colour vision, its sense of smell is at least a hundred times more sensitive than that of humans. A dog's sense of smell tells it as much about its surroundings as its vision does.

Dogs use scents to communicate with each other. Males mark out their territory with urine, which acts as a scent message for other dogs. Males also find a mate for breeding by following the scent left by a bitch on heat (see over page).

Tracking

Bloodhound

Open nostrils

Bloodhounds and German Shepherd Dogs are two of the best tracking dogs because of their very keen sense of smell.

By sniffing the air, dogs can pick up a scent at a distance. They can also follow a scent trail on the ground (and follow it in the right direction) when it is as much as four days old.

Testing the sense of smell

OBJECT WRAPPED IN NEWSPAPER

SMALL PIECE OF MEAT WRAPPED IN NEWSPAPER

MORE OBJECTS WRAPPED IN NEWSPAPER

This is an experiment to show how well a dog can smell. Get a piece of meat and other objects (not food) and wrap them up in newspaper so you have several parcels. See how long it takes the dog to find the parcel with the piece of meat in it.

A first meeting

Two dogs that are strangers will sniff nose to nose. If each can tell from the other's face and tail that it is friendly, they will stand head to tail sniffing each other's bodies. They will remember each other in future by these "scent pictures".

Marking territory

Second scent mark

First scent mark

Third scent mark

A male dog claims an area as his territory by lifting his back leg and urinating on convenient objects like trees or lampposts. These act as scent-markers for his territory. Often several dogs will claim the same territory, especially in crowded towns. Each dog will then leave his urine on the same scent-markers, aiming at the right height to cover up the scent marks of the other dogs. In a pack of dogs only the leader marks out a territory. If another dog in the pack urinates on the leader's marker, the two dogs will fight for the pack leadership.

Scraping

The dog's solid waste carries a scent produced by a special gland under the tail. This gives the dog another way of marking territory. It will often scrape the ground beside its droppings, not to bury them, but to draw attention to the scent mark. As it scrapes, glands between the claws may also leave a scent.

Sweat trail

Dogs can sweat only through their paw pads. The sweat leaves a scent trail on the ground which other dogs can follow.

New smells

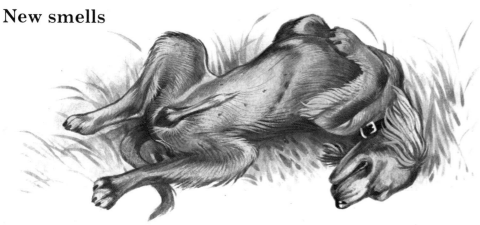

Dogs often roll in cow pats and other strong-smelling things. They probably do this to try and make their own dog-smell stronger.
  Wearing a strong smell seems to be important to a dog because other dogs will then recognize it as superior. In a pack, all the lesser dogs will carefully sniff a pack member "wearing" a new smell.

New objects

A dog will investigate any new object by smelling it thoroughly all over.

Courtship and mating

Dogs usually become sexually mature when they are six to twelve months old. Two or three times a year the female has "heat periods". This is the time when she can mate with a male dog and become pregnant.

Do not be frightened if you notice drops of blood coming from your dog's vulva. This is perfectly normal and is one of the signs that she has come "on heat". She can become pregnant during the two weeks following the period of bleeding. She can also mate with two different dogs in one heat period, which will give her a mixed litter of puppies.

If a male is afraid or feels unsettled because he is in a strange place, he may refuse to mate. This is why the bitch is often taken to the male to mate.

You should only let a bitch have pups if you know you have time to look after them and can find them good homes. If you do not want her to get pregnant she can be neutered, or spayed, at any age after five months. This is a simple operation in which the vet removes her internal sex organs. Male dogs can also be neutered.

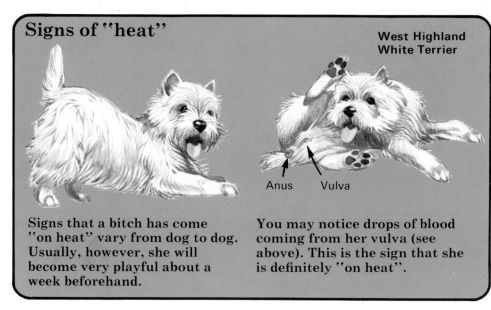

Signs of "heat"

West Highland White Terrier

Anus   Vulva

Signs that a bitch has come "on heat" vary from dog to dog. Usually, however, she will become very playful about a week beforehand.

You may notice drops of blood coming from her vulva (see above). This is the sign that she is definitely "on heat".

Attracting a mate

Bulldog

Cross-breed

West Highland White Terrier

Dachshund (Smooth-haired)

When a bitch is on heat, her urine contains a special chemical. When male dogs smell this in the urine, they know that she is ready to mate. During this period it is not a good idea to take a bitch for walks, as she urinates more often, and will soon be followed by male dogs who have smelt the chemical in her urine.

Dogs of different sizes and breeds can mate together, but if a large male mates with a small female, the bitch may have trouble giving birth to the puppies.

Courtship behaviour

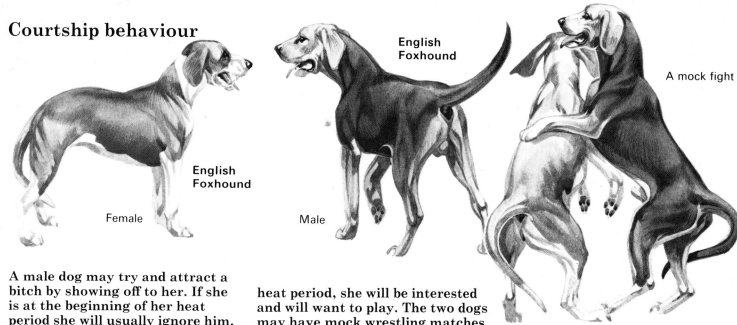

English Foxhound

English Foxhound
Female

Male

A mock fight

A male dog may try and attract a bitch by showing off to her. If she is at the beginning of her heat period she will usually ignore him, but if she is near the middle of the heat period, she will be interested and will want to play. The two dogs may have mock wrestling matches and will sniff and lick each other.

Mating

Male

Female

Dogs in a "tie"

The bitch signals she is ready to mate by moving her tail to one side and showing her vulva to the male. She will stand still as he mounts her from behind, holding on to her middle with his front legs. Although the male dismounts, the dogs still stay joined together (called the "tie") for up to half an hour. This is quite normal and does not hurt them, so do not try to separate them. Afterwards they will clean themselves and the bitch will become playful again.

Pregnancy

1 Signs to look for

Cocker Spaniel

Signs that a bitch is pregnant start to appear about six weeks after mating. Her nipples get larger and the shine of her coat improves.

2 Food

Good food is important for a pregnant bitch. Feed her more as she starts to show signs of pregnancy. She will need up to twice as much food as usual.

3 Rest

During her pregnancy, which lasts about 62 days, the bitch will take less exercise and will spend more time resting, often lying on her stomach.

The birth and care of puppies

If a dog is about to give birth to puppies (this is called whelping), she needs a special whelping box in a warm, quiet, fairly dark place. When the bitch is ready to give birth, her behaviour changes. She becomes restless and will probably refuse to eat. However, she may feel hungry after whelping, so some food should be offered then.

It is best that only one person stays with the bitch while she is whelping, so as not to distract her. A small dog usually has a litter of four to six puppies, but a large dog may give birth to as many as ten. The puppies arrive every 20 to 60 minutes, and as each one is born, the mother licks it clean and eats all the waste matter. Later on, she also licks up the puppies' urine and solid waste to keep the nest clean.

For the first week or so, the mother stays close to the puppies and will not leave them on their own for very long. If disturbed by lots of visitors, she may get worried and accidentally injure her pups while trying to hide them.

1 First signs

A few hours before her puppies are born, the bitch will start to sniff all around the whelping box. She will scratch at the floor as if trying to make a nest.

2 The birth

The bitch usually lies on her side or front to give birth. The puppies may be born head or back legs first. Each one is enclosed in a thin sac full of water.

3 The birth

If the thin water sac has not broken during the birth, the bitch licks it off so that the puppy can breathe.

4 Licking clean

As she licks the puppy clean, it starts to squeak and wriggle about. It moves its head from side to side and turns itself the right way up.

5 Suckling

Each puppy crawls around until it finds a teat, pushing the fur out of its way with its nose. The puppies feed every two hours, sleeping in between. The first ones to stir wake the others, so they all feed together.

Cocker Spaniel

Sleeping pup being woken by its wriggling brother. None of the puppies' eyes are open yet.

Pup kneads with front paws to make the milk flow.

Pup pushes on back legs to brace itself.

Finding the teat

1 Newborn puppy crawling around the nest to find a teat.

2 Puppy burrowing into a hand.

A newborn puppy needs its mother for food and warmth, but it cannot see or hear. It finds her body by touch, changing direction as it crawls about, and moving its head from side to side trying to feel her. Whenever its head touches something, its mouth searches for a teat.

In its search for food, a puppy will burrow into anything soft and warm. It will nose into your hand just as it does into its mother's fur.

Starting to explore

1 Puppies are more active after two weeks. Their eyes open, but they cannot see properly.

2 At 16–18 days old, sense of smell develops. The puppies now start to sniff at everything.

3 The puppy now explores with its tongue, licking itself, other puppies and human hands.

5 Puppies start playful fighting at about three weeks old. They gnaw and bite each other.

4 Hearing develops at about 21 days. The pups will be frightened by sudden, loud noises.

For the first two weeks of its life, a puppy spends most of its time feeding and sleeping, and takes little notice of the other puppies in the litter. In the third week it slowly begins to explore, sniffing, licking or gnawing things around it. At 21 days it can see and hear properly. The puppies now play games together and are ready to move outside their box.

Growing up

The puppies move out of the whelping box after about three weeks. They start spending less time with their mother.

From four to twelve weeks is a very important age because it is now that the puppy forms its impression of the outside world and learns how to react to other dogs and humans. The experiences it has during these weeks shape its behaviour as an adult dog. It is best to buy a puppy at 6 to 12 weeks old, so that you can help it to start developing good behaviour at this vital stage by handling it.

The pups start to explore and investigate everything within reach.

Older pups feed in a sitting position, while the mother stands. A raised paw is used as a gesture of friendship by adult dogs.

If the pups are hungry they may nudge the mother's mouth.

The pups start to take soft foods from a bowl.

Keeping a record

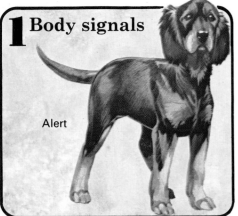

If your dog has pups, it is a good idea to keep a notebook on their progress. Try to weigh them regularly.

As the puppies grow stronger they move about more. They feed outside the box, and also urinate away from it, so it stays cleaner. This is the time to start house training. The mother is becoming less willing to feed them as their teeth and claws start to scratch her, so they can now start feeding on milk and soft foods.

1 Body signals

Alert

A dog signals its intentions or feelings to other dogs and people with its body. It may change from this alert position to become friendly, angry or frightened.

2

Friendly and playful

A dog in this friendly, begging pose is asking another dog or its owner to play with it. It may also lick, or nudge with its nose, to try and get someone to play.

3

Wanting to play or to be forgiven

Another signal to play is when a dog raises its forepaws, one after the other. It also does this when it is asking to be forgiven, or to be stroked.

Playing together

Puppies enjoy playing tug-of-war games, with each other and with people, using a rag as their "prey".

Making friends

From six to twelve weeks old, a puppy should have frequent contact with people, otherwise it will grow up shy and will be difficult to train.

Forming a pack

At four months old pups have a group order, running down from the leader to the most inferior pup.

The games that the puppies play change all the time, but various fighting games are the most common. Through fighting, chasing and stalking games, the puppies practise behaviour which will be useful to them when they are adult dogs.

The strongest puppy in the play group will usually grow up to be a superior or leader dog in an adult group.

4 Apologetic and submissive

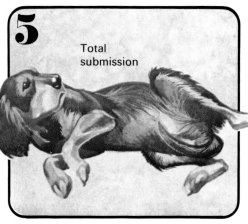

This is a submissive position, with the tail between the legs. A dog will behave like this if it has been scolded, or if it is frightened of a person.

5 Total submission

Dogs roll over like this as a sign of giving in completely (total submission). A puppy may do this to a stranger. It may even urinate, but should not be punished.

6 Fear

A dog may show this fear posture in new surroundings or if there are changes at home. It also shows this behaviour if it thinks it is about to be punished.

Dogs as pets

If you want a dog as a pet, you should first work out how much spare time you will have to be with your dog. As a puppy it will need to be played with and trained. Is there enough space and money for it to be looked after properly? Can you cope with the miles of free exercise that some hunting dogs need? Or would you rather have a dog that is happy running about in a small garden? Are you prepared to groom a long-haired dog? Think how much it will cost to feed a large dog. Do you want a puppy or a fully grown dog, a male or a female?

Remember that most dogs were originally bred as working dogs, and even if kept as pets, they will still want to use their inbred working abilities.

Once you have decided on a breed, find out all you can about it from a specialist breeder, from books and other owners, before buying a dog.

Never buy a puppy on impulse. Never bring a new pet home at Christmas. The noise and excitement will make it very difficult for the animal to settle happily in its new home.

Mongrel or pedigree?

Pedigree dog   Mongrel

A pedigree dog has ancestors all of the same breed, recorded for at least three generations. A mongrel is a mixture of breeds.

Which breed?

There are more breeds of dog than of any other domestic animal. They vary enormously in the kind of care needed to keep them fit and happy. Here are some points to help you choose a breed.

Cocker Spaniel
Long-eared dogs need special grooming to keep ears clean and healthy.

Standard Poodle
Poodles do not moult, but need clipping once every six weeks. First bred as retrievers so are active, trainable dogs.

Afghan Hound
Hounds need plenty of free exercise daily. Long-haired dogs need regular grooming.

Irish Wolfhound
Very large dogs may need a kennel outside, but they also need human company in the daytime.

Basset Hound
A heavy dog that needs a lot of space. Bred to hunt hares, so likes a lot of exercise.

Scottish Terrier
Most terrier breeds are very energetic and need a lot of attention. May dig up the garden.

Papillon
Toy dogs get enough exercise in small gardens and cannot cope with long walks. More fussy over food than large breeds.

Which puppy?

Bottom puppy
(too timid)

The pup to choose

Top puppy
(too self-willed
and noisy)

Health

Bright, clear eyes

Full set of teeth

Healthy coat

Choose your puppy when it is six to ten weeks old. Go to a person who breeds dogs rather than a petshop, so that you will be able to have a look at the mother as well.

Watch the litter for some time to see how they all behave. Do not choose an obvious leader because it could be hard to train. Make a loud noise and notice how each pup reacts. The bottom pup will be nervous and cower in a corner. Choose one that is confident and interested in you.

Check that your pup is healthy before buying it. Look at its teeth, ears and eyes. Ask the owner if it has had any injections yet.

Do's and don'ts

Here are some hints to help you when you bring your new pup home. Remember that for the first few days it needs lots of quiet, sleep and care.

DO GIVE THE PUP ITS OWN FOOD AND DRINK BOWLS. FEED REGULARLY, FOUR TIMES A DAY. GIVE THE PUP A PLASTIC BASKET OR CARDBOARD BOX AS A BED, WITH NEWSPAPER AND AN OLD BLANKET. KEEP IT AWAY FROM DRAUGHTS

DON'T HOLD BY SCRUFF OF NECK AFTER FIRST FEW WEEKS – THE PUP IS TOO HEAVY

DON'T LEAVE SMALL OBJECTS OR ELECTRIC FLEX LYING AROUND – THE PUP MAY BITE OR SWALLOW THEM

DON'T BEAT THE PUP – SCOLD IT WITH A STERN VOICE OR A GENTLE TAP WITH A FOLDED NEWSPAPER

DON'T LEAVE IN A HIGH PLACE – THE PUP MAY HURT ITSELF BY JUMPING DOWN

DO HOLD THE PUP FIRMLY – NOT TIGHTLY – TO STOP IT JUMPING FROM YOUR ARMS

DO GIVE THE PUP A LARGE BONE OR RUBBER TOY TO PLAY WITH

DO TAKE PUP TO THE VET FOR VACCINATION AND WORM PILLS

DO START HOUSE TRAINING EARLY USING NEWSPAPER AND TAKING PUP OUTSIDE. BE PATIENT

Training your dog

All dogs need some training, not only for road safety reasons, but to keep them happy. In the wild, dogs, like wolves, would live in packs. Each pack would have a pack leader. In a human family, the dog's owner is the pack leader, and the dog expects to obey him.

Only one person should train a dog. When you start training lessons do not make them too long and never lose patience with your dog. Praise it when it behaves well. Try and make the lessons into games, so that the dog will enjoy learning.

Basic training

1 House training

A pup sniffs the floor, and circles when it is about to urinate.

Start to house train your pup as soon as possible. At eight weeks, a pup needs to urinate about twelve times a day, but especially after meals and after walking and playing.

When your pup wants to urinate, place it gently on some newspaper. During the next few weeks, move the paper closer to the back door, and eventually into the garden, until the pup asks to be let out.

The first commands

1 Heel

First get the pup used to walking on the lead. Keep it on your left. When it is used to the lead say the word "heel" as you start to walk. If it pulls away, jerk it back and repeat the command "heel".

2 Sit

To train the puppy to sit when you tell it to, push it into a sitting position by pressing gently on its hindquarters, saying "sit" as you do so. You can encourage it with a small food reward.

During short, frequent lessons, slowly progress to saying "sit" before you push the pup down. If you use a hand signal when saying "sit" you can soon teach it to obey just the hand signal.

3 Come

Teach your puppy to come on command by saying "come" when it is about to come to you anyway. Then walk away and call it to you. Finally stay still and call. Give it praise when it comes to you.

4 Wait and come

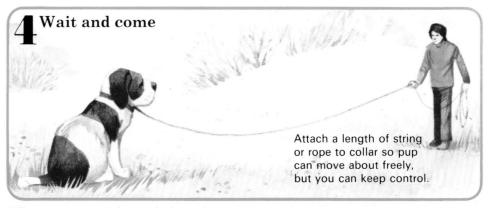

Attach a length of string or rope to collar so pup can move about freely, but you can keep control.

When your pup obeys the word "sit", you can teach it to "stay". Tell it to sit, then move slowly away, backwards. If the pup starts to move, repeat the "sit" command. Stop after a short

distance and call the pup to you. Praise it when it comes. Each time you do this, slowly increase the distance between you and the pup, and teach it to wait for longer periods before calling "come".

2 The first words

Use a friendly voice, and praise and fondle to reward good behaviour. Say the pup's name and "yes" when it does the right thing. Always try and use the same words and tone of voice when praising.

Use the pup's name and "no" to scold it. Use a deep, stern voice. Only scold during or straight after the event—it is no good being cross later, as the pup will have forgotten its bad deed.

3 Wearing a collar

The puppy's collar should be a soft, lightweight one. It should not be too tight, but neither should it be so loose that the puppy can pull its head free.

Further training

1 Fetch and come

Training can be made into a game. Throw a stick for your pup to fetch, but keep it to heel until you give the command "fetch". Run towards the stick to show the pup what you want it to do. If it does not pick it up, put the stick in its mouth. Call the pup back to you and gently take away the stick.

2 Tracking

Scent trail

Most puppies enjoy tracking games. Put your scent on a ball by rubbing it in your hands. Let your pup sniff the ball, then tell it to sit while you walk away and hide the ball. Trample on the grass as you walk, so that you leave a scent trail. Return to the pup and tell it to "seek". Help it to follow your track by pointing in the right direction.

Looking after your dog

Feeding is an important part of looking after your dog. In the wild, although dogs might eat huge meals, they would not feed regularly and would have lots of exercise. A pet dog, which is fed regularly and has limited exercise, does not need large meals. Give your dog a balanced diet and avoid sweet things. If you want to give a reward when you are training your dog, give it a small piece of cheese or a dog biscuit.

Grooming your dog is also important, to keep its skin clean and healthy.

Feeding

There are three main types of dog food to choose from (1, 2 or 3 in this picture).

Feeding a puppy

Start to wean a pup at about three weeks. Give it soft foods. Start with four meals, then cut down to one or two meals a day at seven months.

Weighing

To weigh a small dog, weigh the dog and yourself together, then subtract your own weight. With a larger dog, try and get it to sit on the scales.

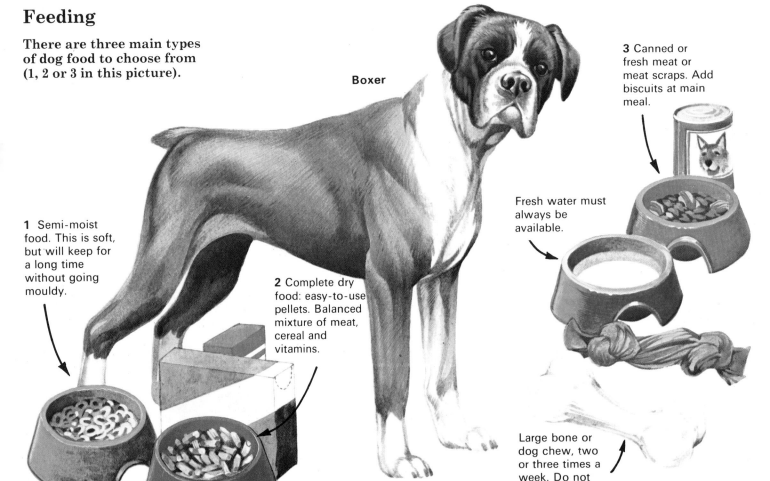

Boxer

1 Semi-moist food. This is soft, but will keep for a long time without going mouldy.

2 Complete dry food: easy-to-use pellets. Balanced mixture of meat, cereal and vitamins.

3 Canned or fresh meat or meat scraps. Add biscuits at main meal.

Fresh water must always be available.

Large bone or dog chew, two or three times a week. Do not use chicken or other small, splintery bones.

Dogs need only one or two meals a day. The amount of food they need depends on their weight and age, and the amount of exercise they have. Hard-working, or growing dogs, for example, will need more than older, less active ones. Most dogs will eat more than they need, so only give your dog enough to keep it at a healthy weight. Check its weight regularly. Always follow the instructions on prepared foods.

Grooming

Old English Sheepdog

Try and get into the habit of grooming your dog regularly every day. This is much better than the occasional long session. Find out which comb, brush and glove to buy for your breed. Use the comb to remove tangles and dirt, then brush the coat from head to tail to remove dead hair. Shine the coat and massage the skin with a hound glove (the bristly surface for long hair, the velvet for short hair).

Poodle clipping

Poodles, and some Terriers, need special clipping every six to eight weeks because they do not moult.

Basset Hound

Bristle brush
Brush coat following the direction of the coat.

Bristle brush

Metal comb
Use to comb through coat.

Hound glove
Use to shine the coat.

Two coats

Puli

The Hungarian Puli sheepdog, like many other breeds, has a thick woolly undercoat and a long outer coat. Any tangled ringlets of hair should be untangled with the fingers.

Bathing

Use dog or baby shampoo with warm water when bathing a dog. Dry it well and don't let it go straight out into the cold. In hot weather, large dogs can be sponged down outdoors.

Clipping claws

Cut here

Walking on hard surfaces like pavements usually wears down a dog's claws. However, some dogs may need to have their claws cut so they do not grow around into the foot pad.

Out of doors

Car journeys

Dalmatian

Your dog should be taught to get in and out of a car only on command, so that it does not leap out immediately a door is opened. If you have to leave the dog in the car, always leave a window slightly open. Make sure the car is in the shade.

It is dangerous to allow a dog to hang its head out of the window while the car is moving. This also makes its eyes sore.

In the country

In general, large dogs need more exercise than small ones. If a dog is well trained and will come when called, a free run is the best exercise. Off the lead a dog will cover far more ground than with its owner. Keep it on the lead in traffic, on lanes without footpaths, and in the country where there are farm animals around.

Collars and leads

A slip chain is useful for training large, strong dogs. Put it on like this.

Wrong

WARNING! MAKE SURE YOU PUT SLIP CHAIN ON CORRECTLY OR YOU MAY CHOKE YOUR DOG

All dogs must wear a collar, with the owner's name and address on a disc.

A lead of leather, nylon or chain with a leather handle.

Make sure your dog's collar fits properly. There should be just enough room to slip two fingers between the collar and its neck.

Holidays

If you need to leave your dog in a boarding kennel, book a place well before your holiday. To help it settle, take its own rug and a favourite toy.

Whistling

A dog whistle is useful for calling your dog. The whistle makes such a high note that only dogs, and some children, can hear it.

Illness and injury

All puppies must be vaccinated against distemper, hepatitis, jaundice and nephritis, and given booster injections once a year. If your dog shows signs of illness, it is best to see a vet. Follow his instructions carefully, and do not use medicines without his advice.

If a dog is injured in a road accident, move it to a safe place and call a vet. To move the dog, lay a blanket or old coat behind its back and pull it gently on to the blanket with its legs trailing. Hold the blanket like a stretcher to carry the dog away.

Common problems

1 Worms

A pup with a pot belly may have worms.

Roundworms and tapeworms are common parasites in dogs and puppies. Look out for small whitish worms in their solid waste. The vet will tell you which medicine to use.

2 Fleas and lice   (These are shown greatly enlarged.)

Grey **lice**, which suck the dog's blood, may be found clinging to the skin, especially on the ear flaps.

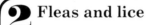

Shiny brown **fleas,** 1–2 mm long, may be found in a dog's fur, often on the back near the tail.

The fleas' powdery, black droppings may irritate skin.

A dog that keeps scratching or biting its skin may have fleas or lice. If you find signs of these insects in the dog's fur you can treat them yourself with a dog powder. Follow the instructions carefully, especially if you are treating a puppy. You should also wash bedding, and bath and groom the dog regularly.

Rabies

Rabies is a dangerous disease that can pass from dogs to people. It occurs in many countries, so if you go on holiday abroad, keep away from stray dogs.

Ears

Dogs with long ears suffer from ear troubles more than short-eared ones. If your dog shows signs of pain or irritation in the ear, take it to the vet. Never poke into the ear yourself.

Flat-faced breeds

Pug

The folds of skin on flat-faced breeds may become sore because they are not open to the air, so keep the folds clean and dry. Some short-faced breeds may also have breathing **difficulties**.

More dogs to spot

This chart shows some popular breeds; you will find more inside the book. Remember that dogs of the same breed can sometimes be different colours. The dogs shown here are not drawn exactly to scale. The average height of a male dog, measured from the shoulder, is given next to the name.

Toy dogs

Pekingese
20 cm

Chihuahua
22 cm

Italian
Greyhound
31 cm

Cavalier King Charles Spaniel
35 cm

Chinese Crested
Dog
34 cm

Maltese
23 cm

Yorkshire
Terrier
20 cm

Griffon
Bruxellois
26 cm

Pug
31 cm

Gundogs

Labrador Retriever
56 cm

English Springer
Spaniel 51 cm

Irish Setter
61 cm

Golden
Retriever
58 cm

Hungarian Vizsla
59 cm

American Cocker
Spaniel 38 cm

German
Short-haired
Pointer
61 cm

Working dogs

Great Dane
90 cm

Welsh Corgi (Pembroke)
28 cm

Collie
(Rough)
58 cm

Newfoundland
71 cm

Belgian Shepherd
Dog (Groenendael)
62 cm

Hounds

Finnish Spitz
48 cm

Borzoi
74 cm

Basenji
43 cm

**Dachshund
(Long-haired)**
25 cm

Whippet
47 cm

Terriers

**Australian
Terrier**
26 cm

**Fox Terrier
(Wire)**
39 cm

**Scottish
Terrier**
27 cm

**Cairn
Terrier**
28 cm

Jack Russell
31 cm

**Bull
Terrier**
40 cm

Utility dogs

**Miniature
Schnauzer**
35 cm

**Chow
Chow**
51 cm

**French
Bulldog**
36 cm

Miniature Poodle
33 cm

Dalmatian
58 cm

**German
Shepherd Dog**
64 cm

**Pyrenean
Mountain Dog**
76 cm

Boxer
56 cm

Dobermann
69 cm

Briard
64 cm

Sacred and mythical dogs

Anubis

Anubis was a god of the ancient Egyptians who, they believed, guided the souls of the dead to the underworld. He could appear either as a dog, or as a human with a dog's or a jackal's head. They believed that Anubis stood guard over tombs, protecting the mummified bodies against a monster who waited to eat them.

Anubis

The Mexican dogs

Mexican pottery dog

This pot is in the shape of a Mexican hairless dog. The ancient Mexican Aztec Indians believed that a soul could reach the underworld only if it was led by the spirit of a dog. Sometimes they buried the body of a hairless dog with a human corpse.

Dog men

When Marco Polo travelled in India he recorded an ancient tale about strange "dog men." Apparently the Indians believed that people from the Adaman Islands all had dogs' heads. They were believed to be savage fighters who ate any prisoners taken during battle.

The black phantom dog

From Europe and North America come many tales of the black phantom dog. It was supposed to be as big as a calf, with a shaggy, black coat and blazing eyes the size of saucers. To see the dog or hear its terrifying howl was often an omen of death.

Witches

In the Middle Ages many people believed in witches. Records from witch trials mention dog "familiars." These were messengers of the devil, disguised as dogs and sent to help the witch with her black magic. They were summoned only at moments of extreme danger.

Cerberus, the Hound of Hell

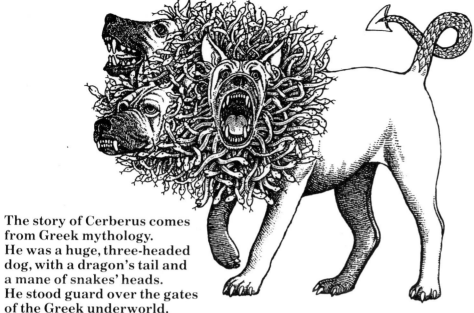

The story of Cerberus comes
from Greek mythology.
He was a huge, three-headed
dog, with a dragon's tail and
a mane of snakes' heads.
He stood guard over the gates
of the Greek underworld.

Faithful dogs

The legend of the faithful dog
has been recorded in many
countries. A Welsh version tells
of the tragic day that Prince
Llewellyn left his dog Gelert
to guard his baby son.

On returning, he found the baby
missing and blood everywhere.
Believing that Gelert had eaten
the child he killed him. Too late,
he found the child safe, hidden
from view by the body of a wolf,
which had been killed by Gelert.
In memory of the dog, a special
grave was made. Today the burial
place is still called Beth Gelert.

The legend of the Dog Stars

The legend of Orion and the
Dog Stars comes from Greek
mythology. It tells how Artemis,
the goddess of hunting, fell in
love with Orion, a Greek giant
and hunter. Her brother, the
sun-god, was so jealous that he
tricked her into killing Orion.
Determined to make him
immortal, Artemis carried
Orion and his two favourite
hunting hounds up to the stars.

Today you can still see the
Orion group of stars. At his feet
is Sirius, the greater Dog Star,
(the brightest star in the sky)
and at his shoulder Maera, the
lesser Dog Star.

Dogs and medicine

Japanese puppy charm

In Japan, the puppy is a symbol
of good health. New babies are
given puppy charms.

In ancient Greece, sacred
dogs were often kept in the
temples of Asklepios, the god of
medicine. They were trained to
lick sick people and were
believed to cure many of them.

The African medicine dog

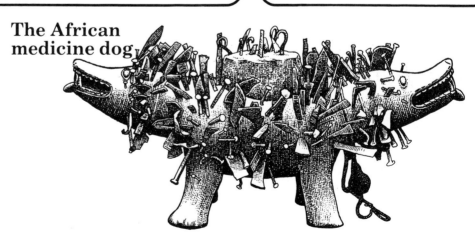

Until recent times the peoples of
Zaire still used wooden medicine
dogs like the one above. Inside each
two-headed dog lived a spirit. If a
man was ill he could get rid of the
illness by asking the spirit to give it
to an enemy. The spirit was released
to do his work by the hammering of
a nail or blade into the dog's back.

Part 3

Hereford cow

Part 3 written by
Ruth Thomson

New Hampshire cock

Embden goose

Landrace pig

FARM ANIMALS

This section will help you to understand how farm animals behave. It shows how farmers' work is influenced by the animals' behaviour, so that, for example, pigs are put in farrowing crates for the first few days after the birth of their piglets (see page 75), and goats' paddocks must have strong, high fences built around them (see page 86). It also shows how the animals' behaviour is affected by farming methods. For example, chickens are

encouraged to lay more eggs than they would normally by keeping them in a windowless shed with the lights left on for about 17 hours a day (see pages 78-79).

If you would like to find out more about farms and farm animals, one of the best ways is to visit a farm. Some farms have open days, when the public are welcomed by the farmer and shown around the farm. There may be one such farm in your area, or you could

ask a local farmer if he would mind if you spent some time on his farm. Show him this book, and tell him that you understand about shutting gates etc. (see page 69), and that you would like to find out more for yourself by observing the animals.

If you visit a farm or go for walks in the country, you can use this book to spot the different breeds of farm animals; there are charts on pages 92-93 and 94-95 which will help you identify them.

British Alpine goat

Farms and farming

No-one knows exactly when animals were first used by man. Cattle, sheep and goats were probably tamed thousands of years ago by hunters who followed grazing herds. As time passed, people thought of the herd they hunted as their own, and learned to control it.

Eventually, the animals became quite tame. People still killed some of them for their meat and hide, but they also learned how to milk them and how to spin and weave sheeps' and goats' wool into cloth. In this way, people could have food and clothes without killing so many of their animals.

It was hard work following the animals on foot. Gradually, the herdsmen tamed some of the larger animals, such as horses, reindeer, camels and yaks. Then they could ride from pasture to pasture with their herds.

When people settled down to farm, they kept animals not only for food, but also to help them farm. Oxen pulled carts and ploughs and animal dung was used to manure the soil, so that crops grew well.

Pigs and poultry were tamed by farmers who lived near forests where these animals were found.

Once all these animals were tamed, people kept on trying to breed only the ones which they thought were the most useful. This is called selective breeding. People have succeeded in breeding cattle with shorter, meatier hindquarters that give better beef, cows that give more milk, sheep with heavier fleeces, and hens that lay more eggs.

Over the centuries, farm animals have often, through breeding, changed shape and colour.

Where did farm animals come from?

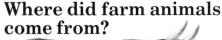

Most cattle breeds can be traced back to wild **aurochs**. These large, fierce, agile animals once lived in herds in parts of Europe, Asia and north Africa.

Many different kinds of **wild sheep** used to live in mountain areas. They were tamed for their meat and wool.

Farm ducks are descended from wild **mallard ducks**.

Grey farm geese are descended from wild **greylag geese**.

Chickens are descended from the **wild jungle fowl** of south-east Asia.

Turkeys come from north America, where they were first kept by the Indians.

Farm pigs are descended from **wild boars**, which still live in parts of Europe, Asia and north Africa.

Useful words

	Full-grown male	Full-grown female	Castrated male	Young female	Baby
Cattle	Bull	Cow	Bullock	Heifer	Calf
Sheep	Ram	Ewe	Wether	Hogg	Lamb
Chickens	Cock	Hen	Capon	Pullet	Chick
Pigs	Boar	Sow	Hog	Gilt	Piglet

This chart shows you the names given to male and female animals at different times in their lives. Male animals are sometimes castrated: this means that they have an operation soon after they are born, which prevents them from mating or reproducing. Castrated animals put on weight more easily when they get older and are less aggressive.

DO'S AND DON'TS ON THE FARM

DO KEEP TO FOOTPATHS OR THE EDGES OF FIELDS

DO KEEP YOUR DOG ON A LEAD – IT MAY RUN AROUND AND FRIGHTEN THE ANIMALS

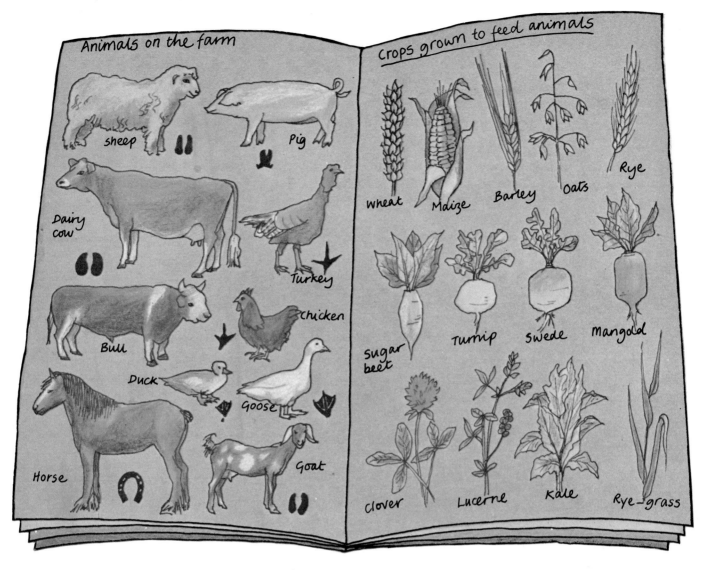

Make your own farm scrapbook

When you visit or go for a walk near a farm, look out for things to collect and keep in a scrapbook. As well as drawing the animals you see, watch out for bits of hair or wool caught on fences or hedges, feathers on the ground, and animals' tracks in mud. Then try to match them to the animals they came from.

You could also collect or draw different crops and find out which animals they are fed to. If you see several different breeds of one animal, use the chart further on in this book to find out what they are.

Cattle

Cattle are the most important domestic animals. They can change grass, which has little food value for people, into milk, which is rich in food value. They can do this because they have four stomachs to digest the food. Cattle, goats and sheep all digest their food in the same way, and are called ruminants.

Some breeds of cattle are kept for their meat, others for their milk, and a few breeds are kept for both. In some countries, cattle are used for ploughing or for pulling carts.

Cattle do not have upper front teeth. They eat by wrapping their tongues around grass and pulling it into their mouths. They use their back teeth for chewing the cud (see over the page).

In most breeds, cows as well as bulls have horns. The horns are usually cut off when the cattle are young, so that they cannot hurt one another. Some breeds, known as "polled" cattle, never have horns.

Most cattle have coats of thick, short hair. Some which live in cold climates have long hair to keep them warm. The skins of cattle can be made into leather.

Jersey cow

Cows have an udder with four openings called teats. Milk is produced in the udder after the cow has given birth. The calf sucks the teats to get the milk.

Teat

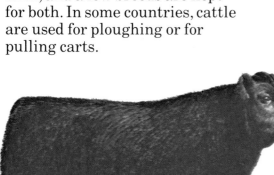

Aberdeen Angus cow

Beef cattle have broad, fleshy hindquarters, a thick neck and short legs. They look almost rectangular in shape.

Hoof print

Cattle are cloven-hoofed animals. Their tracks show the two toes which make up each hoof.

Dairy cattle look bonier than beef cattle. Their udders are bigger and hang lower. They have long legs and slim hindquarters. They look wedge-shaped from the side, because the body tapers towards the head.

Cow-watcher's guide

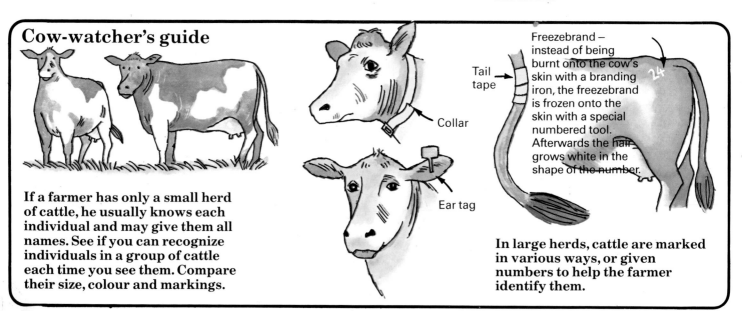

If a farmer has only a small herd of cattle, he usually knows each individual and may give them all names. See if you can recognize individuals in a group of cattle each time you see them. Compare their size, colour and markings.

Collar

Ear tag

Tail tape

Freezebrand — instead of being burnt onto the cow's skin with a branding iron, the freezebrand is frozen onto the skin with a special numbered tool. Afterwards the hair grows white in the shape of the number.

In large herds, cattle are marked in various ways, or given numbers to help the farmer identify them.

Breeding calves

Hereford bull

Bulls are never kept with other males because they are aggressive and would fight. Some bulls are kept in fields and others in bull pens at the farm.

A cow "in calf" (pregnant)

A cow can have calves when she is two years old. When she is ready to mate, she is said to be "in season". Forty weeks after mating, she gives birth to one, or occasionally two, calves.

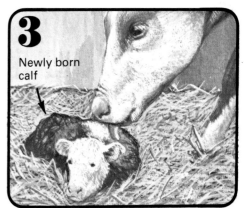

Newly born calf

A new-born calf weighs 25-45 kg. It has curly hair which grows straight when it is about one week old. It can stand up when it is only two hours old, and then tries to find a teat.

Calf suckling

The cow licks and nudges the newborn calf to help it find a teat. The calf wraps its tongue around the teat and sucks hard to get the milk. It often butts the udder, and this may help increase the milk flow.

Herefords

Very young calf

Calves of dairy cattle are taken away from their mothers (see over page), but calves of beef cattle can stay with the cows because the farmers do not need the milk. At first the cow grazes around her calf, but as it gets older, she grazes further away. If a cow loses her calf, she calls loudly until she finds it. The calf may try several cows before it finds its mother.

6

Older calves form groups away from their mothers, except when they are suckling. They chase and run about together.

One calf will often sniff a resting calf and then push it with its nose to make it get up and play.

Calves sleep close together, lying down.

Calves have mock fights, pushing their heads together.

Calves are very curious. They sniff strange objects and then lick them.

Cattle

Fighting

When they are young, cattle may threaten one another to establish leadership. A threatening cow stands with its head lowered and its hind legs forward, eyeing its rival. Sometimes it will paw the ground.

If the other cow makes a threat too, they fight. They try to knock one another and push with their heads. Fights end when one cow loses interest and walks away.

Leading the herd

In an established herd, there is usually a particular cow which always leads the others when they are going in to be milked. It is not necessarily the strongest or

Food

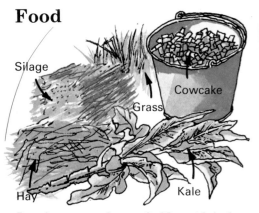

Silage

Grass

Cowcake

Hay

Kale

In winter, cattle are fed hay (dried grass) or silage (pickled grass) and sometimes kale (a sort of cabbage). Throughout the year, they are also fed cow cake, made of barley, soya, fish meal and molasses (sugar).

Drinking

Cows need about 60 litres of water per day. They drink most after evening milking. They keep their nostrils above the water's surface while they are drinking.

Grazing and grooming

Cattle use their tails to flick off flies and to brush their skins.

While chewing, a cow moves its head about looking for the next patch of grass to eat. It may walk about 4km a day.

How cattle eat

Cattle swallow grass without chewing it properly. It goes into the rumen, where it is stored and broken down into balls of cud. When the cow has eaten its fill, it rests and "chews the cud". The balls of cud are brought back up into the mouth, are chewed into a pulp, and then reswallowed. In the reticulum, some food is stored and any bits of metal or stone are trapped. The pulp is strained in the omasum; any undigested food goes back to

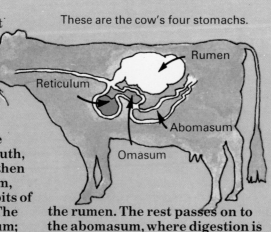

These are the cow's four stomachs.

Rumen

Reticulum

Abomasum

Omasum

the rumen. The rest passes on to the abomasum, where digestion is completed.

oldest cow: in fact, the older cattle are normally at the back of a moving group, along with the weaker ones.

Milking

Milking machines copy the action of the hand. In hand-milking, the dairyman grasps a teat in each hand and squeezes it with his thumb and forefinger. Then he gently but firmly pulls his hand down the teat to get the milk out.

The cow's year

The amount of milk a dairy cow produces varies from month to month. A cow does not produce any milk at all until the first calf is born. The farmer removes the calf two days after birth, so that the cow is free to be milked.

She is milked twice a day to keep the milk yield high and is given extra food. The cow is milked for ten months. Within three months after calving (giving birth), she is mated again.

During pregnancy the milk yield falls gradually, and for two months before the birth, the cow is "dry". For six weeks before the birth, she is given extra food to help her produce a good milk supply after calving. This is called "steaming up".

Starting with the month when a calf was born, make a calendar showing how a cow's milk yield changes over a year. Write at the top of the calendar the name of the cow, its age and any special features you notice about it.

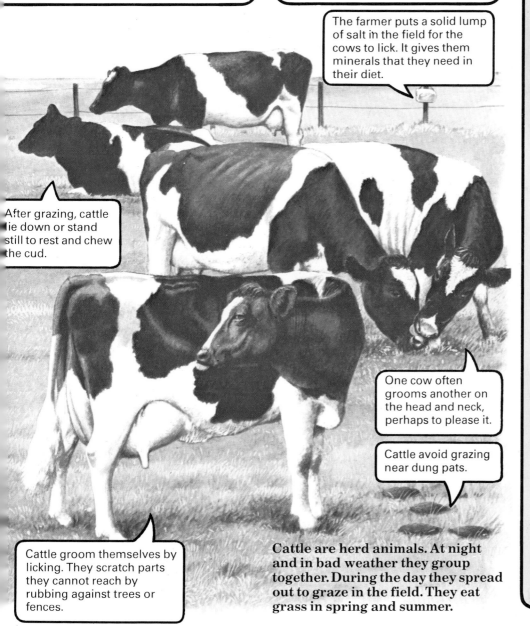

The farmer puts a solid lump of salt in the field for the cows to lick. It gives them minerals that they need in their diet.

After grazing, cattle lie down or stand still to rest and chew the cud.

One cow often grooms another on the head and neck, perhaps to please it.

Cattle avoid grazing near dung pats.

Cattle groom themselves by licking. They scratch parts they cannot reach by rubbing against trees or fences.

Cattle are herd animals. At night and in bad weather they group together. During the day they spread out to graze in the field. They eat grass in spring and summer.

Name : WISDOM MAYQUEEN
Breed : JERSEY
Age : 2 YEARS
Date of birth of 1st calf : 1/9/78

Month	Event	Milk * Yield
Sept	1st calf born, milk production starts	22
Oct		22
Nov		20
Dec	Cow mated with bull	19
Jan	cow in calf	12
Feb	"	14
March	"	12
April	"	12
May	"	9
June	"	6
July	cow is "dry"	none
Aug	"steaming up"	none
Sept	2nd calf born	22

* Amount produced in one day of each month, in kilograms

Pigs

Pigs may be kept either indoors or outdoors. Pigs used for breeding are often kept outdoors in fields. The pigs can run about and search for food, although the farmer will also feed them. Their active life keeps them strong and healthy.

Pigs kept for their meat (pork, bacon and ham) are usually kept in pens. They are fed controlled amounts of food, such as wheat, barley, potatoes, corn, fish meal and skimmed milk. The pigs do not use much energy and become fat. Their bristles can be made into brushes.

Wild boar

Tusk

Snout

The wild pigs from which domestic pigs were bred once roamed the woodlands. They ate acorns, roots and worms, which they dug out of the soil with their snouts (this is called "rooting"). The pigs lived in herds of females and their young. The boars (males) joined them for the mating season.

Living outdoors

Electric fence

Drinking trough

Shelter

Saddleback sow

Feeder

Pigs cannot sweat. In hot weather, they wallow in wet mud and sleep stretched out to cool themselves.

Fenced-in food area for piglets.

Landrace sow

Pigs are very clean animals. They sleep in one place, which is kept clean and dry, and excrete in another.

Even in a pen like this one, pigs will root for food in the ground. If the farmer does not want the soil churned up in this way, he will put a metal ring through the pig's nose to stop it rooting.

Food pellets

Landrace boar

Living in a piggery

Sows (female pigs) can produce more than two litters a year and have between 10 and 14 piglets in each litter.

Young female pigs (called "gilts") are first mated at the age of eight months. Gilts of one breed are often mated with a boar of a different breed to produce cross-bred pigs, which grow faster and are often healthier than pure-bred pigs.

The gilts give birth (known as "farrowing") 16 weeks after mating.

1 Making a nest

A few days before a sow is due to farrow, she is put in a farrowing pen. The farmer puts down straw, which the sow paws into a heap.

Sows that give birth outdoors find a hollow and line it with chewed-up leaves and straw to make a warm, dry nest.

2 Giving birth

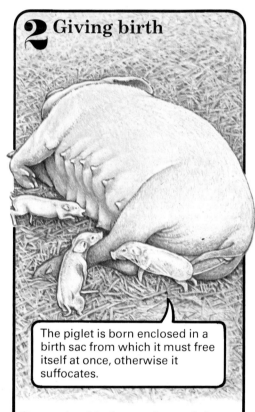

> The piglet is born enclosed in a birth sac from which it must free itself at once, otherwise it suffocates.

Sows give birth mostly at night. A few hours beforehand, the sow lies down and loudly grunts and squeals. Just before each birth, she swishes her tail and may kick and lift her leg to help force a piglet out.

The newborn piglets can walk a few minutes after birth and stagger round the sow's hind legs, looking for a teat to suck for milk.

The temperature of the udder is particularly high, and the piglets huddle around it to keep warm as well as to feed.

3 Young piglets

Dunging area

Farrowing crate

Infra-red light provides heat

> The last piglet born is often so weak and small that it cannot survive. It is known as the "runt".

Farmers keep the sow in a farrowing crate like the one above for about four days, until the piglets are nimble enough to keep out of her way as she lies down. The warmth of an infra-red light attracts the piglets away from the sow. Piglets are very sensitive to cold and huddle under the light, their limbs tucked under their bodies. This keeps them safely out of the way of the sow, who might otherwise crush them. When they are hungry, the piglets creep under the rails of the crate to suckle milk. After a week, they are given sweet food, which at first they play with but soon learn to eat.

4 Feeding and playing

Fenced-in feeding trough for piglets.

The piglets often have mock fights. They bite one another on the face and ears. Farmers cut the piglets' sharp teeth so that they cannot damage the sow's teats or one another.

The front teats give more milk than the back ones, so the piglets at the front are usually heavier than the ones at the back.

The piglets each settle on one particular teat and return to the same one for every feed. If the sow rolls over onto her other side, the teat order is upset and the piglets fight for their new positions. If the litter is so large that there are more piglets than teats, some piglets will not manage to find a proper place in the teat order.

When the piglets are about one week old, several sows and their piglets are all put in a large pen together. This is called a multi-suckling unit. The piglets get used to one another while they still feed from their mothers. Sometimes they even feed from other sows. If the litters were not mixed until the piglets were much older they would fight.

While the piglets are young, they feed about once an hour. The sow lies down and grunts to let the piglets know she is ready to feed them. They gather at her teats and jostle for a position at one of the teats, squealing and biting one another.

First, they push the teats with their snouts to help release the milk. They suckle until the milk stops flowing and then nose the teats again to make more milk flow.

5 Weaning

Pigs learn to press a metal plate, called a nipple drinker, with their snouts when they want some water.

If pigs are bored or overcrowded in pens, they may bite one another's tails. Farmers often hang up a tyre or a chain for them to play with instead.

After about six weeks, the piglets eat solid food and no longer need their mother's milk. This is called weaning. The sows are taken out of the pen and the young pigs are put in an area called a weaner pool. They run about together until they weigh about 50 kilograms. Then, graded according to size, they are put in fattening pens.

Even in small pens, pigs keep their sleeping and food areas clean. They always excrete in another part of the pen. Some pens have dunging alleys, in which the pigs learn to excrete.

How fast do pigs grow?

(A **fully mature pig** of one year weighs about 170 kg.)

If you can visit a farm where there are pigs, you could make a chart like this to show how fast a pig grows. Look at the pigs carefully and draw pictures of them at different ages. Put the age of the pig under each picture. Notice how their shape changes.

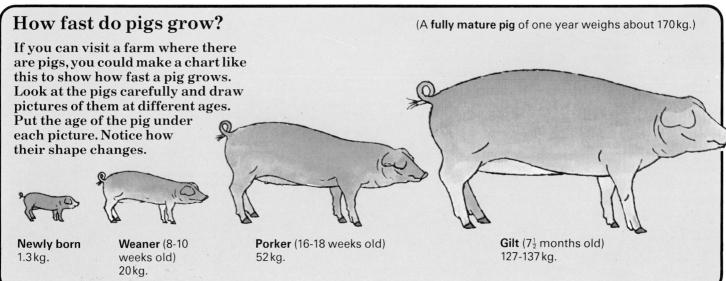

Newly born
1.3 kg.

Weaner (8-10 weeks old)
20 kg.

Porker (16-18 weeks old)
52 kg.

Gilt ($7\frac{1}{2}$ months old)
127-137 kg.

Chickens

Farmers keep poultry either for eggs or meat. Poultry farming is a very specialized business and most chickens are reared and kept indoors. Broiler (meat) chickens are kept in windowless sheds with a controlled amount of light. As many as 20,000 chicks will be put together in one shed. They are given plenty of rich food and are killed at about nine weeks old.

The pictures on these pages show three methods of keeping hens for egg-laying: free range, deep litter and battery houses. Chicks which are going to one of these three places are kept in a heated shed called a brooder at first. When they are about five months old, the pullets (young birds) are ready to lay eggs. They lay most of their eggs in their first year, and are often sold for boiling in their second year.

Hens normally lay eggs which are unfertilized (which means no chicks will grow in them). If a farmer wants to produce chicks, rather than eggs to eat, he has to mate his hens with a cock. They then will lay fertile eggs.

Incubator

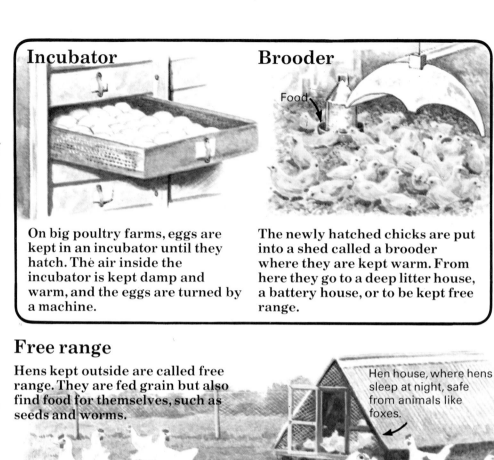

On big poultry farms, eggs are kept in an incubator until they hatch. The air inside the incubator is kept damp and warm, and the eggs are turned by a machine.

Brooder

Food

The newly hatched chicks are put into a shed called a brooder where they are kept warm. From here they go to a deep litter house, a battery house, or to be kept free range.

Free range

Hens kept outside are called free range. They are fed grain but also find food for themselves, such as seeds and worms.

Hen house, where hens sleep at night, safe from animals like foxes.

Free range hens lay a different number of eggs according to the season. They lay most in the spring when the days are lengthening and fewest in the autumn when there are fewer hours of daylight each day.

How chicks are born

1 Cock displaying to a hen

With modern methods of poultry keeping the hens' "natural" behaviour is not often seen. These pictures show how chicks are born when the hens are allowed to mate and lay eggs on their own. Before mating, a cock performs a courtship

2 Hen laying an egg

display for a hen. He may waltz around her with his ruff raised and one wing held out. If the hen wants to mate, she will crouch and allow the cock to mount her.

After mating, the hen finds a dark, dry place in which to make a nest of

3 Hen incubating her eggs

straw and lay the eggs. When she is about to lay, she clucks, ruffles her feathers and squats over the nest. After laying, the hen sits tightly on the eggs to keep them at the same heat as her body, about 41°C. This is called incubation. She turns the

Deep litter

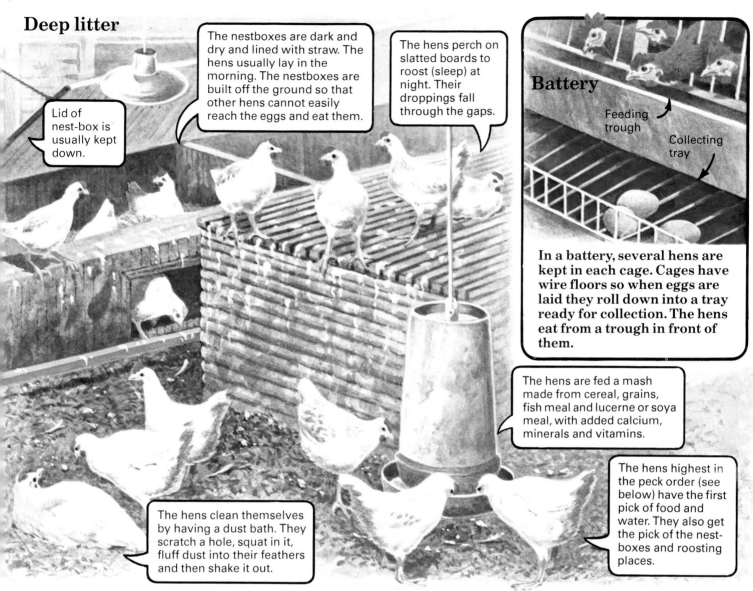

Lid of nest-box is usually kept down.

The nestboxes are dark and dry and lined with straw. The hens usually lay in the morning. The nestboxes are built off the ground so that other hens cannot easily reach the eggs and eat them.

The hens perch on slatted boards to roost (sleep) at night. Their droppings fall through the gaps.

The hens clean themselves by having a dust bath. They scratch a hole, squat in it, fluff dust into their feathers and then shake it out.

Battery

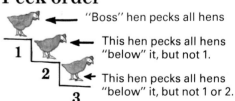

Feeding trough

Collecting tray

In a battery, several hens are kept in each cage. Cages have wire floors so when eggs are laid they roll down into a tray ready for collection. The hens eat from a trough in front of them.

The hens are fed a mash made from cereal, grains, fish meal and lucerne or soya meal, with added calcium, minerals and vitamins.

The hens highest in the peck order (see below) have the first pick of food and water. They also get the pick of the nest-boxes and roosting places.

Deep litter houses are windowless and lights are left on for about 17 hours a day. This encourages the hens to lay the largest possible number of eggs all year round.

The floor is usually concrete and is covered with straw or wood shavings.

Hundreds of hens are put together in one house. Like battery hens, they never go out of doors. The tips of their beaks may be cut to prevent them from pecking one another.

4 Chick hatching out

Egg tooth

eggs over several times a day to keep them evenly warmed.

The chicks hatch after 21 days. They break through the egg-shell with their egg tooth and push themselves out. They stand up and shake their down dry. Young chicks

5 Chicks pecking for food

still need warmth. The hen covers them with her wings at night. The chicks peck wherever their mother pecks and in this way, learn what to eat.

Peck order

"Boss" hen pecks all hens

1 This hen pecks all hens "below" it, but not 1.

2 This hen pecks all hens "below" it, but not 1 or 2.

3

Hens have a system known as a "peck order" by which all the hens in a group are ranked according to their aggressiveness. The hen at the top of the "ladder" is the one that pecks all the others most and is recognized by them as the "boss". The next hen down pecks all the others "below" it, but not the one "above" it. Each hen occupies a certain position on the "ladder".

Turkeys, Ducks and Geese

Turkeys can be kept together in large numbers. They need careful attention because disease can spread easily. If frightened, turkeys gobble loudly and huddle in a corner on top of one another. The ones at the bottom of the pile may be smothered.

Ducks and geese are hardier and are kept outside. They have an oily film on their feathers which keeps their bodies dry when they swim. They can survive quite well without a pond, but they like a lot of water to dip their heads in and to throw over their backs.

Ducks and geese

Farm ducks and geese are much heavier than their wild relations. They can fly only near the ground and for very short distances. They group together when foraging for food.

In summer both ducks and geese moult. Their down feathers are sometimes used to stuff pillows and quilts.

Turkeys

Females

Male

Turkeys have food available all the time and eat as much as they want. In 26 weeks from hatching a turkey can grow to about 13 kilograms.

Males perform a courtship display where they spread their feathers, strut and make a noise (called "gobbling").

Geese are easily disturbed. They raise their heads and honk loudly.

Geese crop grass very closely. Sometimes farmers keep them in orchards to keep the grass down.

If a goose feels threatened, for example by a dog, it lowers and stretches its neck forward and hisses. The gander (the male) comes forward to protect the other geese.

Ducks are driven in here for the night. Geese have a separate hut.

Ducks eat grass and farmers feed them grain. They also eat waterweed, seeds and fruits of water plants, snails, slugs and worms.

Ducks up-end like this in deeper water in search of food.

Ducks preen themselves by rubbing a gland near the tail with their bills to pick up oil which they spread over their feathers.

Ducks dabble for food in shallow water. They dip only their head and neck in the water.

Poultry

What is an egg?

Chicken   Duck   Turkey   Goose

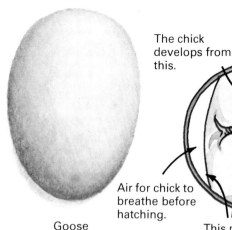

The chick develops from this.

Air can pass through the shell for the chick to breathe.

These "chalaza" hold the yolk in place and act as shock absorbers.

Air for chick to breathe before hatching.

This membrane prevents the chick from sticking to the shell.

The yolk is very rich food for the growing chick.

The egg white provides water for the growing chick and kills germs that pass through the shell.

Chickens, ducks, geese, turkeys and guinea fowl are known as poultry. All poultry lay eggs, which vary in colour and size. Some examples are shown above. In the wild state, the birds would lay a clutch of eggs and sit on them until they hatched. Farmers take the eggs away as soon as they are laid, so the birds keep on laying.

Chicken

Gosling

Duck or goose eggs are often given to hens to hatch. A hen cannot tell the difference between these and her own eggs, even though they take longer to hatch.

Chicken

Gosling

Chicks follow the first moving object they see on hatching. Goslings and ducklings will adopt the hen who incubated them as their mother.

Test an egg's freshness

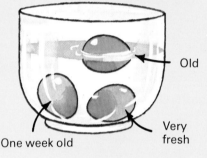

Old

One week old

Very fresh

Put a teaspoonful of salt in a bowl of cold water. Place an egg in it. You can tell how old it is by the way it floats or sinks.

Beaks and feet

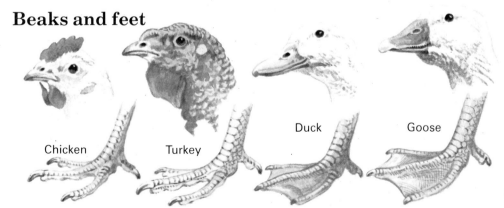

Chicken   Turkey   Duck   Goose

Chickens and turkeys have feet with sharp claws, and can scratch for food and grip branches. They have sharp beaks for pecking grain and other seeds. Ducks and geese have webbed feet for swimming. Their flat bills have a tooth-like edge which is good for grazing. Ducks have a sort of comb in their beaks which sieves snails and other animals from mud and water.

How birds eat

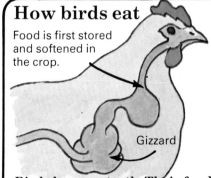

Food is first stored and softened in the crop.

Gizzard

Birds have no teeth. Their food goes down into the crop, a kind of bag, just below the gullet, and is then ground up by the gizzard, a muscular sac. Poultry are fed grit with their food to help this grinding process.

81

Sheep

Sheep are timid animals that live in flocks. They copy one another and usually they all eat together and rest together.

There are many different breeds of sheep, each of which has been bred to suit a particular region. For example, the sheep on this page have been bred to live on rich lowland pastures; the ones on the opposite page have been bred to survive on hills and mountains. Some breeds of sheep can live in quite hot climates and withstand drought; others survive in areas where the ground is cold and wet. In some countries, sheep are kept indoors much of the time.

If sheep of a breed living in one area were taken to another area with a completely different climate and pasture, the quality of their wool and meat would quickly change and they might even die.

Lowland sheep

Lowland sheep are usually kept in fenced fields and most breeds are larger than hill sheep, with shorter, thicker fleeces (wool coats). The lambs fatten quickly for meat.

Most lowland breeds, when they produce lambs, have twins or even triplets.

As well as eating grass, lowland sheep often forage in hedges for weeds, which are a small but important part of their diet.

Sheep often eat all facing the same way, and always with the wind blowing towards them. Each sheep usually keeps two others in view while eating.

Sheep have front teeth on only the lower jaw, so they cannot bite properly. Instead, they tear the grass by jerking their heads forward and upward. They crop the grass very closely.

Dorset Down sheep

Sheep groom only their faces. They lick their foreleg and then rub their face with it.

Hill sheep

Hill sheep are hardier than lowland sheep and can live on poorer pasture. They are more agile because they spend so much of their time moving up and down hills and over rocky ground.

All hill sheep have coarse, often long, wool which protects them from the harsh climate.

A hill flock divides into groups, each with its own particular feeding area. Since the sheep rarely stray out of this area, farmers do not need to fence them in. When a lamb grows up, it stays in the same feeding area as its mother.

Hill sheep always return to the higher slopes at night. They graze back down to the lower slopes during the day.

Sheep follow definite paths called "sheep walks" across the hills between grazing sites, drinking places and rest places.

Sheep move in groups, following one another in single file. They are usually led by an old ewe. They walk with their heads down unless they are alarmed. Then they raise their heads and ears, bunch together and run away.

Sheep are brought down to the pasture around the farm (known as the "in-bye" lands) for shearing, dipping and veterinary treatment. They always come down to the lower slopes for lambing.

Hill ewes usually have only one lamb a year. Their food is not rich enough to produce milk for more than one lamb.

In summer, sheep rest near water and shade. Resting places are easy to spot because dark green weeds and clover grow around them. Sheep never sleep deeply, like dogs or cats do; they rest mainly at night.

Rough Fell sheep

Hill sheep eat heather and other shrubs as well as grass. They drink from streams and ponds.

The sheep's year

In late summer, the shepherd checks over his flock. Sheeps' hooves grow all the time and normally wear down as the sheep move around. The shepherd has to trim the hooves if they have not worn down, otherwise the sheep become lame. He also looks for infections in the feet.

The teeth are checked, because as sheep grow older their teeth wear down to stumps and some drop out, making it difficult for the sheep to eat. Sheep that cannot eat are no use to farmers and are sold for mutton.

Finally, the shepherd inspects the ewe's udders to make sure that they will be able to feed lambs properly. Most ewes can mate only in the autumn. Rams, which are kept in a group separate from the rest of the flock, are turned out with the ewes at this time. Each ram will mate with up to 60 ewes.

It is important that the rams get on well together, so that they do not frighten the ewes by fighting. Usually, one of the older rams is the leader of the group. A new ram may challenge and fight the leader until it finds its place in the group.

When two rams fight they butt and charge each other.

3 Lambing

Newly born lamb

Ewe butting away another ewe's lamb.

A ewe gives birth 150 days after mating. As soon as the lamb is born, the ewe gets up to lick it dry. She learns to recognize it by its smell.

A lamb takes three or four days to learn to recognize its mother. It may try to suckle other ewes but they will butt it away.

4 Lambs

Young lambs frolic around their mothers.

When lambs are a few days old, the shepherd may remove their tails. This is called "docking" and is done to prevent disease. A long tail would get dirty.

Sheepdogs

Sheep are very timid animals and respect sheepdogs. On hill farms, or where sheep range over a large area, it would be very difficult to move them from place to place without the help of dogs.

Sheepdogs have a natural herding instinct but do have to be trained to obey the shepherd's orders. Their main task is to gather the flock together and drive them in the right direction. A good dog can also divide a flock up or separate out a single sheep.

The shepherd calls or whistles orders to his dog.

The dog circles the sheep to gather them together. He can then drive them wherever the shepherd wants.

1 Raddling

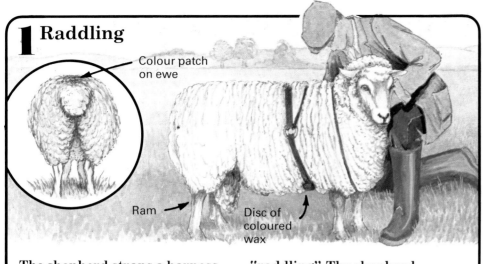

Colour patch on ewe

Ram

Disc of coloured wax

The shepherd straps a harness with a piece of coloured wax attached to it around the ram's chest. When the ram mates with a ewe, he leaves a smear of the colour on her rump. This is called "raddling". The shepherd changes the colour of the wax every three weeks. He can then tell roughly when a ewe will have lambs from the colour left on her by the ram.

2 Winter feeding

Over the winter, and especially before lambing (the birth of the lambs), ewes are given extra food such as hay, oats or barley.

Older lambs play together.

At about three weeks lambs start to become adventurous and form play groups. They race and have mock fights. Ewes call their lambs by bleating.

5 Shearing

Newly shorn sheep

As the weather gets warmer, the ewes naturally shed their wool. Farmers shear the wool before this happens and sell the fleeces.

6 Dipping

Once or twice during the year sheep are dipped in a bath of insecticide. This protects the sheep from diseases and parasites.

How to spin wool

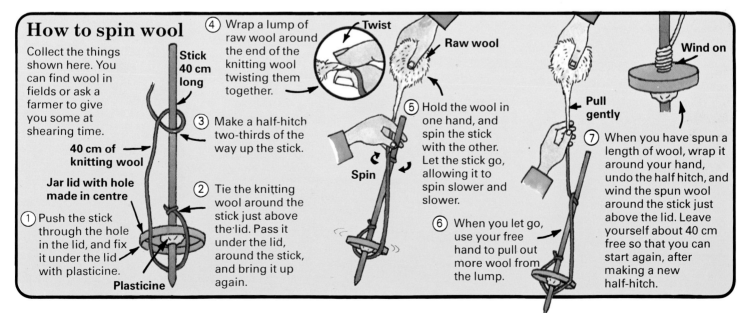

Collect the things shown here. You can find wool in fields or ask a farmer to give you some at shearing time.

Stick 40 cm long

40 cm of knitting wool

Jar lid with hole made in centre

① Push the stick through the hole in the lid, and fix it under the lid with plasticine.

Plasticine

② Tie the knitting wool around the stick just above the lid. Pass it under the lid, around the stick, and bring it up again.

③ Make a half-hitch two-thirds of the way up the stick.

④ Wrap a lump of raw wool around the end of the knitting wool twisting them together.

Twist

Raw wool

Spin

⑤ Hold the wool in one hand, and spin the stick with the other. Let the stick go, allowing it to spin slower and slower.

⑥ When you let go, use your free hand to pull out more wool from the lump.

Pull gently

Wind on

⑦ When you have spun a length of wool, wrap it around your hand, undo the half hitch, and wind the spun wool around the stick just above the lid. Leave yourself about 40 cm free so that you can start again, after making a new half-hitch.

Goats

Goats give a plentiful supply of milk, which is much easier to digest than cow's milk, so many people keep just a few goats for that purpose.

Like cows and sheep, goats are ruminants, which means they can store food in their rumen and rechew it later.

Some goats are kept in pens or paddocks, and others are allowed to wander freely over mountainsides or scrub land.

Some breeds are also kept for their wool, or for their skin, which is very soft.

British Alpine

Male goats are bigger and shaggier than females. All males have beards which grow longer as the goat gets older. They have a very strong smell, especially during the breeding season.

All goats, males and females, can have horns, but some may be born with none. Usually, the horn "buds" (which look like small knuckles) are removed by a vet when the kid is about four days old. If the goat is going to be tethered in a place where it might get attacked by dogs, its horns are kept as a defence.

Goats kept in a paddock

Goats kept in pens or paddocks are milked twice a day and are fed hay and concentrate (a mixture of bran, oats, maize, etc.) They may also eat grass and other plants. Their owners exercise them to keep them healthy, and every month the goats' hooves are trimmed with special shears.

Goats can jump over heights of 1.5 metres. They will eat through hedges and butt holes in wire netting, so goat-keepers build high fences to prevent goats from escaping.

Goats are browsers rather than grazers. They like to nibble the tips of saplings, young shoots and the bark of trees. If not prevented, they will eat right through hedges and destroy them.

Goats usually give birth to two or three kids at one time. Most male kids are killed at birth; a few are kept for breeding. All kids are taken from the mother when they are four days old to be bottle-fed, so that the mother can be milked by the goat-keeper. When the kids are three to four weeks old, they are returned to the herd.

Mountain goats

People often keep a herd of goats on mountain-sides or on land that is too poor, too steep or too hot for cattle and sheep. Led by a goatherd, the goats are allowed to roam about and may wander up to 20 kilometres in a day.

There is always a leader of the herd, usually the oldest female. Goats cannot be driven, unlike sheep and cattle. If a goatherd wants to move the goats, he takes one or two of them and leads the way. The others will then follow.

In the Alps, the goats are milked in the morning, taken up to the grassy slopes for the day, and brought down to a shelter for the night.

Goats dislike rainy, muddy conditions. Goat-keepers usually provide them with a house to shelter in. Ideally, each goat has a pen with straw bedding and a hayrack on the wall.

Goats have a very good sense of balance. They are sure-footed and can walk along narrow ledges and climb jagged rocks.

Goats that can wander freely will browse on a mixture of plants including bramble, dandelion, thistles, nettles, hogweed and rosebay.

Kids are very playful and often fight, particularly over food. They butt their heads together.

Pure Toggenbergs

Horses

Some farmers keep horses to help them with their work. On very large farms, horses are essential for herding and rounding up sheep and cattle. Only a few are still used for ploughing.

Some breeds of horses are gentle and easy to handle and some are bad-tempered, but most horses are intelligent and have good memories. They are easy to train and will work hard for their owner. They are also stronger and faster than other farm animals and can carry heavy loads or pull carts or ploughs.

Ploughing

The tail is usually cut short, so that it does not trail in the mud or get caught in the harness.

Draught horses have short, thick necks and wide bodies.

Shire horse

The long hair, called "feather", which grows below the horse's knees, protects its legs from mud.

Horses used for ploughing and pulling heavy carts are called draught horses. They are good for heavy work because they are so strong and are usually quiet and steady. The Shire horse is the heaviest; it can weigh up to 940 kilograms.

Carrying loads

Donkeys can carry great weights and are sure-footed, but they can be very stubborn. They have long ears and a short, upright mane.

Pulling

The Percheron is used for heavy work such as pulling carts.

Rounding up

Horses used on large farms for rounding up cattle are called stock horses.

In the stable

Horses turn their ears towards any noise they hear. The ears pricked forward show friendship and curiosity. Ears laid back show fear or anger.

The forelock and mane grow all the time, like human hair. They help to protect the horse against flies.

A healthy horse will always have a shiny coat. Natural grease in the coat keeps the horse warm and dry.
In winter, most horses grow longer coats which protect them against cold weather. A horse must be groomed daily to keep its coat clean and healthy.

Half-door

Horses can see partially behind them without turning their heads. If they are frightened or angry, their eyes open wide, showing the whites.

Haynet

Manger

The tail also grows all the time. The horse uses it to swish flies away.

A horse's front teeth never stop growing. They are continually being worn down. The front teeth are used for cutting grass and the back teeth for chewing it. You can tell a horse's age by the length and shape of its teeth.

Straw

Bucket of water

Horses have long legs and can run fast. A race-horse can run as fast as 64 k.p.h. over a short distance.

Horses' feet, called hooves, have a hard outer layer which grows like our nails. In the wild, this wears down naturally. The hooves of working horses need to be protected against hard surfaces. They are kept trimmed and fitted with metal shoes.

Keeping a horse in a stable is unnatural, but stables are designed so that horses are kept as healthy and contented as possible. Horses in fields spend most of the day eating, so in a stable, a haynet is put on the wall so that the horse can still eat when it wants.

Working horses are given extra energy foods such as oats, barley and horse cubes. These are put in a manger, so that they do not get trampled on the floor.

Horses travel up to 30 kilometres a day in the wild. They need daily exercise or they become lazy and bad-tempered as well as stiff and bored. A bored horse will kick and chew at its stable door and may develop bad habits such as weaving its head from side to side.

A horse is usually kept by itself in a stable. Horses kept together might compete for food and kick one another. The stable has a half-door so that the horse can look out.

Horses

A young horse is called a foal until it is about a year old. The male foals are called colts and the females fillies. When they are a year old, the colts that are not going to be used for breeding are castrated, and are then known as geldings. Non-castrated male horses are called stallions.

If you see a field of horses, they will probably be mares (adult females), geldings and foals. Stallions are never put in a field with other males, as they would fight for control of the herd.

In parts of the field where there have been a lot of horse droppings, the grass grows coarse and dark green. Horses will not eat this grass even if they are hungry, because it is sour. They often graze a favourite patch bare, ignoring the rest of the field. This is why cattle are sometimes put in the same field; between them, the horses and cattle graze the whole field.

Groups of foals often play together. They gallop about the field, chasing one another and having mock fights (kicking, biting and bucking). They are easily frightened and shy away from strange objects.

Young foals stay close to their mother. They suckle for at least six months, although they start eating grass at about two months. Foals begin to play with grass or hay when they are very young, but they cannot chew it as an adult does.

Later, they start to graze properly, but often their neck is too short for their long legs. They have to straddle (or even cross) their front legs in order to reach the ground.

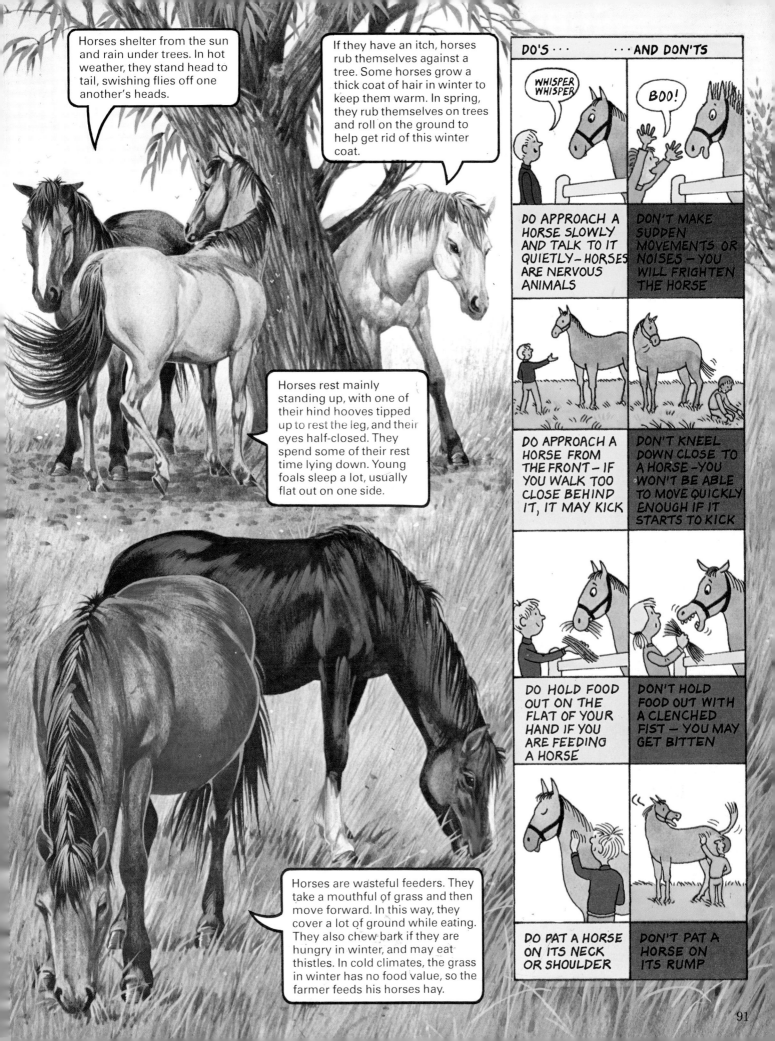

Horses shelter from the sun and rain under trees. In hot weather, they stand head to tail, swishing flies off one another's heads.

If they have an itch, horses rub themselves against a tree. Some horses grow a thick coat of hair in winter to keep them warm. In spring, they rub themselves on trees and roll on the ground to help get rid of this winter coat.

Horses rest mainly standing up, with one of their hind hooves tipped up to rest the leg, and their eyes half-closed. They spend some of their rest time lying down. Young foals sleep a lot, usually flat out on one side.

Horses are wasteful feeders. They take a mouthful of grass and then move forward. In this way, they cover a lot of ground while eating. They also chew bark if they are hungry in winter, and may eat thistles. In cold climates, the grass in winter has no food value, so the farmer feeds his horses hay.

DO'S · · · · · · AND DON'TS

WHISPER WHISPER

BOO!

DO APPROACH A HORSE SLOWLY AND TALK TO IT QUIETLY – HORSES ARE NERVOUS ANIMALS

DON'T MAKE SUDDEN MOVEMENTS OR NOISES – YOU WILL FRIGHTEN THE HORSE

DO APPROACH A HORSE FROM THE FRONT – IF YOU WALK TOO CLOSE BEHIND IT, IT MAY KICK

DON'T KNEEL DOWN CLOSE TO A HORSE – YOU WON'T BE ABLE TO MOVE QUICKLY ENOUGH IF IT STARTS TO KICK

DO HOLD FOOD OUT ON THE FLAT OF YOUR HAND IF YOU ARE FEEDING A HORSE

DON'T HOLD FOOD OUT WITH A CLENCHED FIST – YOU MAY GET BITTEN

DO PAT A HORSE ON ITS NECK OR SHOULDER

DON'T PAT A HORSE ON ITS RUMP

Identifying farm animals

Pigs

Large Black. Kept for pork and bacon. Survives well in hot countries because it does not get sunburnt.

Piétrain. Kept for pork. Low proportion of fat to lean meat. A docile breed, originally from Belgium.

Berkshire. Kept for pork. An old British breed. These pigs mature early.

Gloucester Old Spot. An old English breed. Through breeding, it is gradually losing its spots.

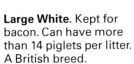

Large White. Kept for bacon. Can have more than 14 piglets per litter. A British breed.

Duroc. Kept for pork. An important American breed with a fast growth rate.

British Saddleback. Kept for bacon and pork. Notice the markings, typical of all Saddlebacks.

Welsh. Kept for bacon. A British breed. Is very hardy and produces large litters.

Middle White. Kept for pork. A cross-breed from the Small White and the Large White.

Tamworth. Kept for bacon and pork. One of the oldest pig breeds; it most resembles the wild pig.

Poland China. Kept for pork. Was bred in United States from the China and Berkshire breeds.

Landrace. A leading bacon breed in Europe. Different countries have developed their own varieties.

Horses and ponies

Clydesdale. Used for general farm work. Has very strong legs.

Shetland. Was once used to haul coal in mines; now used for riding. One of the smallest breeds.

Thoroughbred. The fastest breed, used for riding and racing. Bred from the Arab horse.

If you cannot see the breed of animal you want to identify on these pages, turn to the pages earlier in the book that deal with the relevant animal, and you may see a picture of it there.

Cattle

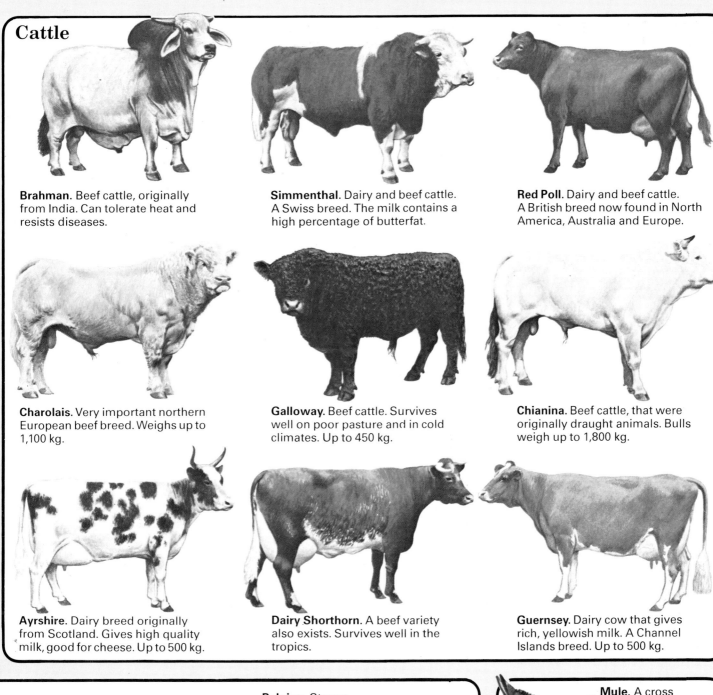

Brahman. Beef cattle, originally from India. Can tolerate heat and resists diseases.

Simmenthal. Dairy and beef cattle. A Swiss breed. The milk contains a high percentage of butterfat.

Red Poll. Dairy and beef cattle. A British breed now found in North America, Australia and Europe.

Charolais. Very important northern European beef breed. Weighs up to 1,100 kg.

Galloway. Beef cattle. Survives well on poor pasture and in cold climates. Up to 450 kg.

Chianina. Beef cattle, that were originally draught animals. Bulls weigh up to 1,800 kg.

Ayrshire. Dairy breed originally from Scotland. Gives high quality milk, good for cheese. Up to 500 kg.

Dairy Shorthorn. A beef variety also exists. Survives well in the tropics.

Guernsey. Dairy cow that gives rich, yellowish milk. A Channel Islands breed. Up to 500 kg.

Quarter horse. Used in North America and Australia for driving cattle.

Belgian. Strong, docile farm horse. Descended from the medieval war horse.

Mule. A cross between a horse and a donkey.

Donkey. Used for riding and carrying loads, especially in the Mediterranean area.

Sheep

Merino. Fine wool. Important in Australia and in the development of other breeds.

Rambouillet. Fine wool. A French breed that resembles the Merino, but is larger.

Southdown. Medium wool. One of the oldest British breeds. Produces good meat and wool.

Ile de France. Long wool. A French breed developed from the Merino. Can lamb in autumn.

Texel. Medium wool. A Dutch breed, whose meat is more important than its wool.

Hampshire Down. Short wool. An English breed with a long breeding season.

Dorset Horn. Medium wool. An English sheep that can breed throughout the year.

Cheviot. Medium wool. A hardy upland breed whose coarse wool is used for rugs.

Welsh Mountain. Long wool. Very hardy sheep, whose wool is used for tweed fabrics.

Border Leicester. Long wool. An English breed, often crossed with hill breeds.

Scottish Blackface. Long wool. A hardy highland sheep. High quality meat.

Corriedale. Long wool. Important in Australia and New Zealand. Meat and wool.

Goats

Toggenberg. Swiss breed. There is also a British Toggenberg which looks similar but is larger.

Anglo-Nubian. A breed developed from a mixture of English and Eastern breeds. Can be any colour with any kind of coat markings.

Saanen. Originally a Swiss breed, but different countries have bred their own varieties. Gives a lot of milk.

British Alpine. This breed was developed from the British Toggenberg.

Chickens *

Rhode Island Red. Brown eggs. Also bred for meat.

White Leghorn. White eggs. Used for developing hybrids.

Barred Plymouth Rock. Tinted (pale brown) eggs.

Light Sussex. Sold for meat. Tinted eggs.

Australop. Pale brown eggs. Developed in Australia.

Indian Game. Sold for meat. Originally from India.

Ross no. 1. Hybrid broiler.

Warren. Hybrid developed from Rhode Is. Red.

Shaver. Hybrid developed from Leghorn.

Ducks

Indian Runner. From Malaya. Can be black, brown or white.

Khaki Campbell. An English breed. The best egg-layer.

Aylesbury. An English breed, kept for its meat. Up to 5 kg.

Muscovy. From South America. Has no voice, only a hiss.

Pekin. A Chinese breed, kept for eggs and meat.

Rouen. A French breed. Plumage looks a bit like a mallard's.

Turkeys

White hybrid. Most common turkey.

Bronze. Once popular but now less common.

Guinea Fowl. From Africa. Has changed little under domestication. Kept for eggs and meat.

Bantam. Small variety of hen. Lays large eggs for its size.

Geese

Toulouse. A French breed. The largest domestic goose. Males and females look alike.

Embden. A German breed. Blue-eyed. Kept for its meat.

*Most laying hens are a cross of several breeds and are known as hybrids. They have been bred to produce more eggs.

Index

Book list

Cats
Practical Guide to Cats. Ivor Raleigh,
Patricia Scott and Elizabeth & Oliphant
Jackson (Hamlyn)
Your Guide to Cats and Kittens. Edited by
Ruth Gardiner (Peter Way)
Cats and Kittens. Jane Rockwell
(Franklin Watts)
Cats. Grace Pond and Angela Sayer
(Bartholomew)
Cats . . . their health and care. TV Vet
(Farming Press)
The Language of Your Cat.
Frank Manolson (Marshall Cavendish)
Cats of the World. Matt Warner (Bantam)
The Observer's Book of Cats. Grace Pond
(Warne)
The Complete Cat Encyclopedia. Edited by
Grace Pond (Crown)

Dogs
Practical Guide to Dogs. Kay White and
Joan Joshua (Hamlyn)
Caring for your Puppy. E. Fitch Daglish
(John Gifford)
The Care of the Family Puppy.
Robert C. White (Popular Dogs)
Dog Training My Way.
Barbara Woodhouse (Woodhouse)
The TV Vet Dog Book. TV Vet
(Farming Press)
Training Your Dog. David Kerr
(Mirror Books)
My Puppy is Born. Joanna Cole
(Lutterworth Press)
Reporter Book Series: Dogs. Werner Kirst
and U. Dierkmeyer (Hart-Davis)
The Dog Directory. Edited by Joe Cartledge
(The Dog Directory)

Dogs of the World. W. R. Fletcher (Bantam)
Dogs of the World in Colour. Ivan Swedrup
(Blandford)

Farm animals
Farming in Britain. Frank Huggett
(A & C Black)
The Observer's Book of Farm Animals.
L. Alderson (Warne)
On Location: Farms. Mary French
(Mills & Boon)
*British sheep breeds, their wool and its
uses.* (From the British Wool Marketing
Board, Oak Mills, Station Road, Clayton,
Bradford, West Yorks, England.)

The Wonderful World of Pets. (Orbis)